THE BEDFORD SERIES IN HISTORY AND CULTURE

The Seven Years' War in North America

A Brief History with Documents

Related Titles in
THE BEDFORD SERIES IN HISTORY AND CULTURE
Advisory Editors: Lynn Hunt, *University of California, Los Angeles*
David W. Blight, *Yale University*
Bonnie G. Smith, *Rutgers University*
Natalie Zemon Davis, *University of Toronto*

THE BEDFORD SERIES IN HISTORY AND CULTURE

The Seven Years' War in North America

A Brief History with Documents

Timothy J. Shannon

Gettysburg College

BEDFORD / ST. MARTIN'S   Boston ◆ New York

For Bedford/St. Martin's

Publisher for History: Mary V. Dougherty
Executive Editor for History: William J. Lombardo
Director of Development for History: Jane Knetzger
Senior Editor: Heidi L. Hood
Executive Editor: Elizabeth M. Welch
Publishing Services Manager: Andrea Cava
Production Supervisor: Victoria Anzalone
Editorial Assistant: Laura Kintz
Project Management: Books By Design, Inc.
Cartography: Mapping Specialists Ltd.
Text Designer: Claire Seng-Niemoeller
Cover Designer: Marine Miller
Cover Art: Courtesy of the Library of Congress Prints and Photographs Division,
    LC-USZC2-1595
Composition: Achorn International, Inc.
Printing and Binding: RR Donnelley and Sons

President, Bedford/St. Martin's: Denise B. Wydra
Director of Marketing: Karen R. Soeltz
Production Director: Susan W. Brown
Director of Rights and Permissions: Hilary Newman

Copyright © 2014 by Bedford / St. Martin's

Manufactured in the United States of America.

8   7   6   5
f   e   d   c   b

For information, write: Bedford / St. Martin's, 75 Arlington Street, Boston, MA 02116
    (617-399-4000)

ISBN 978-0-312-44578-2

Acknowledgments

Acknowledgments and copyrights are continued at the back of the book on page 172, which constitutes an extension of the copyright page. It is a violation of the law to reproduce these selections by any means whatsoever without the written permission of the copyright holder.

Foreword

The Bedford Series in History and Culture is designed so that readers can study the past as historians do.

The historian's first task is finding the evidence. Documents, letters, memoirs, interviews, pictures, movies, novels, or poems can provide facts and clues. Then the historian questions and compares the sources. There is more to do than in a courtroom, for hearsay evidence is welcome, and the historian is usually looking for answers beyond act and motive. Different views of an event may be as important as a single verdict. How a story is told may yield as much information as what it says.

Along the way the historian seeks help from other historians and perhaps from specialists in other disciplines. Finally, it is time to write, to decide on an interpretation and how to arrange the evidence for readers.

Each book in this series contains an important historical document or group of documents, each document a witness from the past and open to interpretation in different ways. The documents are combined with some element of historical narrative—an introduction or a biographical essay, for example—that provides students with an analysis of the primary source material and important background information about the world in which it was produced.

Each book in the series focuses on a specific topic within a specific historical period. Each provides a basis for lively thought and discussion about several aspects of the topic and the historian's role. Each is short enough (and inexpensive enough) to be a reasonable one-week assignment in a college course. Whether as classroom or personal reading, each book in the series provides firsthand experience of the challenge—and fun—of discovering, recreating, and interpreting the past.

Lynn Hunt
David W. Blight
Bonnie G. Smith
Natalie Zemon Davis

*To my colleagues
in the History Department
at Gettysburg College*

Preface

The Seven Years' War was a global conflict, but it is remembered today chiefly because of events in its North American theater, where it had a transformative impact on native and colonial peoples. After more than a century and a half of imperial competition among Europe's great powers, Great Britain and France had emerged by 1750 as the dominant forces in North America. Their dominions, however, were a study in contrasts. French Canada and Louisiana had tiny colonial populations, but the soldiers, fur traders, and Catholic missionaries who lived there had mapped the interior waterways of the continent and formed commercial and diplomatic alliances with the native peoples they encountered. British North America was a mosaic of differing ethnicities, Protestant churches, and colonial governments, rooted along the eastern seaboard yet economically and demographically expansive. Indian nations along the Appalachian frontier were justifiably wary of British western expansion, but they valued the material goods provided by British traders, and they exploited the British colonies as a diplomatic counterbalance to the French.

The story of how the Seven Years' War began in the Ohio country, a remote borderland even to British and French subjects living in North America, has always attracted historians' attention because it involved George Washington's first and very uncertain steps into public life. In fact, the conflict involved many American and British figures who, like Washington, would later play important roles in the American Revolution. But looking ahead to American independence from the perspective of the Seven Years' War is problematic, especially if we rely on stereotypes of haughty British military officers stumbling around in the American wilderness, clinging unsuccessfully to their traditional methods of warfare, while resourceful colonial Americans learned from their Indian allies and enemies how to practice a new kind of warfare adapted to their environment. Making the Seven Years' War a harbinger of the American Revolution also shortchanges the experiences of the non-British peoples swept up in the conflict—the French colonists and soldiers whose lives were permanently disrupted by the British conquest of Canada and the Indian nations whose homelands were the arena of battle.

No one at the time of the Seven Years' War described it as a first step toward American independence, and in many ways it strengthened rather than loosened the bonds between the colonies and Great Britain. A different story unfolds when we examine the war from the perspective of its participants, native and colonial, British and French, soldiers and civilians, men and women. The Seven Years' War brought professional European armies and large-scale military operations to North America, and it engulfed colonial and Native American peoples in unprecedented levels of violence. For many of its participants, the war was a spiritual as well as a military struggle. French Catholics and British Protestants accused each other of perverting Christianity, and in several Indian nations, movements aimed at restoring Native American power by reviving traditional spiritual customs and beliefs took hold. The war also transformed the map of North America, erasing French claims to Canada and Louisiana and leaving the British in control of the continent east of the Mississippi River. Rather than treat the Seven Years' War as a rehearsal for the American Revolution, we can gain a better understanding of it by hearing from the full range of people involved.

In keeping with the goal to treat the Seven Years' War on its own terms, this book opens with an introduction that discusses the war as an intercultural conflict involving Native Americans, French and British soldiers, and the ethnically and religiously diverse population of British North America. The introduction offers a quick, comprehensive overview of the conflict as an international war for empire, but then focuses on events along the northern frontier, where the war originated and had its most important impact for colonists and Native Americans.

The core of this book, its thirty-five primary-source selections, is designed to recapture the experience of the Seven Years' War from multiple perspectives. Source selections offer contrasting views on the Fort William Henry Massacre and the fall of Quebec; they present Native American and European opinions expressed at diplomatic councils; and they recapture the public debate over the war's origins and consequences. We hear representative voices of fur traders, frontier squatters, Indian warriors and diplomats, provincial foot soldiers, captives, and female camp followers, describing their experiences on the early American frontier. Rather than recapitulate chronologically the war's major campaigns and battles, the documents are organized thematically, to address such issues as cultural definitions of warfare, the captivity experience, intercultural diplomacy, and changing notions of savagery and civility. By reading and analyzing these primary sources, students of early American history can gain an appreciation for the ways in which the Seven Years' War reshaped not only the geopolitical map of North America but also the everyday experience of the diverse peoples living within the continent's boundaries.

To aid students' analysis of the sources, each document opens with a headnote that provides historical context and biographical information about the author. Explanatory footnotes appear where useful to clarify the events described. At the end of the volume, students and instructors will find a chronology of the main events of the Seven Years' War in North America, a list of questions suitable for discussion or for writing assignments, and a selected bibliography with suggestions for further reading.

A NOTE ABOUT THE TEXT

History students who read primary sources quickly learn that not only did people in the past think differently than we do today, they wrote differently, too. For the source selections in this book, I have avoided modernizing spelling, capitalization, grammar, and word usage, but I have inserted punctuation and spelled out abbreviations where necessary for clarity.

ACKNOWLEDGMENTS

A number of people helped me bring this project to fruition. I thank David Blight, advisory editor for the Bedford Series in History and Culture, for supporting this volume. Executive editor Elizabeth Welch developed the manuscript and provided expert advice at all stages of production. Many thanks to Beth and her colleagues, including Mary Dougherty, Bill Lombardo, Heidi Hood, Laura Kintz, Andrea Cava, Nancy Benjamin, and Barbara Jatkola. The following reviewers also contributed important feedback, and I thank them for the time and energy they put into their comments: Fred Anderson, University of Colorado Boulder; Patrick Griffin, University of Notre Dame; Daniel Mandell, Truman State University; Paul Mapp, College of William & Mary; Greg O'Brien, University of North Carolina at Greensboro; David Preston, The Citadel; Todd Romero, University of Houston; and John Smith, Texas A&M University–Commerce. For their help as research assistants, I would like to thank Ryan Crooks, Megan Dean, David Fictum, and Caroline Shannon.

At Gettysburg College, Natalie Hinton and Meghan Kelly helped with interlibrary loan materials, and I am grateful to my colleagues in the history department for creating such a collegial environment in which to work and teach. As always, I owe my greatest debt to my family—Colleen, Caroline, Daniel, and Elizabeth—for their love, patience, and support.

Timothy J. Shannon

Contents

PART ONE

Introduction: The Seven Years' War and Cultures in Conflict in North America

On the morning of August 10, 1757, the soldiers and civilians at Fort William Henry prepared for a march to Fort Edward, another British post about sixteen miles away. They were undoubtedly exhausted, maybe even shell-shocked, from having endured a siege by a much larger French army during the previous week.

Fort William Henry and Fort Edward stood at opposite ends of a road connecting Lake George and the Hudson River. These two forts protected British New York from invasion by way of Canada. If they fell, they opened the door to Albany and the lower Hudson Valley, all the way to New York City (see Map 1). Six days earlier, 6,000 French soldiers and 2,000 Indians led by General Louis-Joseph, marquis de Montcalm, had arrived at Fort William Henry. The fort's commander, Lieutenant Colonel George Monro, had a much smaller force of 2,500 British regulars and colonial troops, but he expected reinforcements from Fort Edward and so refused Montcalm's first offer of terms for surrender. The French soldiers went to work around the clock, digging trenches and building batteries that would enable them to move their artillery within range of the fort's walls. Monro's troops tried to slow their advance with fire from the fort, but as the siege wore on, their cannons overheated and split from repeated use.

Monro's hopes for relief were dashed during a meeting with Montcalm on August 7. The French general handed Monro a message taken

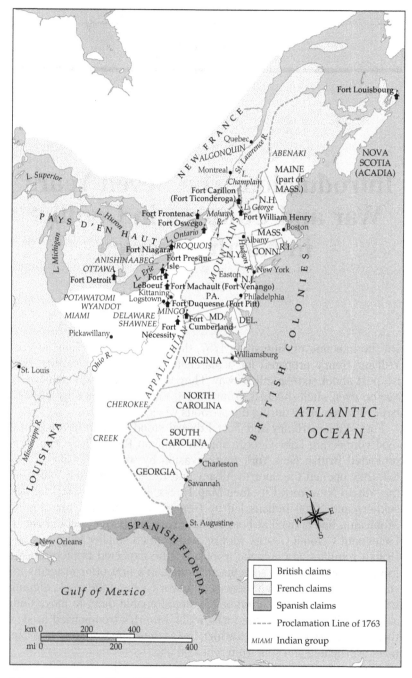

L. Superior

NEW FRANCE

ALGONQUIN

Quebec

St. Lawrence R.

ABENAKI

MAINE
(part of
MASS.)

NOVA
SCOTIA
(ACADIA)

Fort Louisbourg

Montreal

L. Champlain

Fort Carillon
(Fort Ticonderoga)

L. George
Fort William Henry

N.H.

PAYS D'EN HAUT

L. Huron

Fort Frontenac

Mohawk R.

MASS.

Boston

Fort Oswego

L. Ontario

Albany

Hudson R.

CONN.

R.I.

L. Michigan

Fort Niagara

IROQUOIS

N.Y.

ANISHINAABEG

Fort Presque
Isle

MOUNTAINS

OTTAWA

L. Erie

Easton

New York

Fort Detroit

Fort
LeBoeuf

Fort Machault (Fort Venango)

N.J.

POTAWATOMI

Kittanning

Philadelphia

WYANDOT

Logstown

PA.

MIAMI

MINGO

Fort Duquesne (Fort Pitt)

DELAWARE

MD.

DEL.

Pickawillany

SHAWNEE

Fort
Necessity

Fort
Cumberland

Ohio R.

APPALACHIAN

St. Louis

Williamsburg

VIRGINIA

Mississippi R.

CHEROKEE

NORTH
CAROLINA

ATLANTIC
OCEAN

LOUISIANA

CREEK

SOUTH
CAROLINA

GEORGIA

Charleston

Savannah

N

W   E

S

St. Augustine

SPANISH FLORIDA

New Orleans

Gulf of Mexico

BRITISH COLONIES

British claims

French claims

Spanish claims

Proclamation Line of 1763

MIAMI Indian group

km 0   200   400

mi 0   200   400

Map 1. *The Seven Years' War in North America*

2

from a British courier killed while trying to get through the French lines. In the message, Fort Edward's commander, General Daniel Webb, declined Monro's request for reinforcements, explaining that he needed to conserve his forces for defending Albany. He advised Monro to make the best terms he could for surrender. Monro waited two more days in vain, and then finally agreed to hand over the fort to Montcalm on August 9.

Montcalm proved to be a generous enemy. A year earlier, he had led a similar siege against Fort Oswego, a British post on Lake Ontario. The garrison there, however, had put up such a weak defense that Montcalm had refused to grant it the "honors of war," a customary set of concessions that allowed the defeated force to keep its arms and personal property and guaranteed prisoners of war good treatment and rapid repatriation. This time, Montcalm extended the honors of war to Monro, promising protection to the soldiers and civilians under his command in return for their promise not to engage in hostilities against the French for eighteen months. By the code that Monro and Montcalm shared as professional soldiers, both men had acted honorably in this siege, and neither saw any need for further violence or bloodshed.

The Indians who accompanied Montcalm's army were not party to these negotiations, nor had they agreed to the terms of surrender. They practiced a different kind of warfare, with its own cultural rules and conventions. Some of Montcalm's Indian allies came from the *reserves*[1] around Montreal and Quebec, communities of Indians who had submitted to the spiritual instruction of Catholic missionaries and whose proximity to their colonial neighbors had acculturated them to the French way of doing things. Many more were from what the French called the *pays d'en haut*, the western country bounded by the upper Great Lakes, Ohio River, and Mississippi River, where they knew the French as trading partners but otherwise had little familiarity with colonial society. These Indians had traveled far to join Montcalm's force, some several hundred miles, and not because of their curiosity about how Europeans conducted a siege. They had come to build their reputations for bravery and leadership, to acquire plunder and scalps from their enemies, and to take captives. Montcalm and Monro may have felt that the surrender satisfied their need for honor, but it made no provisions for satisfying the Indians' need to bring home tangible proof of their wartime exploits.

What happened next has been recorded in the history books as the Fort William Henry Massacre (Documents 26 and 27). As the column of soldiers and civilians left their encampment and snaked down the road toward Fort Edward, the Indians attacked. Some murdered and

scalped the sick and wounded who had remained behind, too incapaci-
tated to join the rest. Others turned their attention to the column, which
was organized with British regular troops at the head, followed by provincial soldiers and then civilian camp followers at the rear. The regulars marched alongside a French guard provided by Montcalm, but the
provincials and civilians were exposed, unarmed, and panic-stricken.
Warriors stripped clothing and other personal belongings from them,
dispatching those who resisted with tomahawk blows and taking their
scalps. They took more captives and scalps as they pursued individuals who fled into the woods for cover. The column disintegrated in the
pandemonium, making it difficult for French guards to intervene and
restore order. Some warriors, when compelled by French officers to
return their captives, killed and scalped them on the spot.

In a matter of a few minutes, most of the British column had melted
away, as soldiers and civilians ran to the woods, returned to the fort, or
huddled in smaller groups for protection. The dead and dying littered
the ground. One New England soldier who lived through the attack estimated that 1,500 British had been killed or taken captive, well over half
of the fort's garrison. Historian Ian K. Steele, after an exhaustive evalu-
ation of the available evidence, has substantially reduced that number,
estimating that between 70 and 190 British were killed or missing in
action and that 308 were led away into captivity.[2]

If asked today, not many Americans could say much about the Seven
Years' War (except maybe how long it lasted), but their notions about
early America owe much to what happened at Fort William Henry on
that fateful August day. The Fort William Henry Massacre inspired
James Fenimore Cooper's 1826 novel, *The Last of the Mohicans*, which in
turn influenced countless books and films about the American frontier.
In print and on film, *The Last of the Mohicans* depicts colonial America as
an unspoiled but bloody wilderness where the clash between European
civilization and Indian savagery created a new nation. Fenimore Cooper portrayed his Indian characters as the doomed remnants of a dying
race, possessed of a primitive nobility but also driven by an unquench-
able thirst for blood and vengeance. His European characters likewise
fit stereotypical roles. The French are crafty puppet masters of their
Indian allies. British army officers are blundering martinets, disdain-
ful of their colonial subordinates but hopelessly conventional in their
approach to American warfare. The women are British damsels in distress, and the hero, frontiersman Natty Bumppo, is the model colonial
American: independent in spirit and mind, resourceful and brave, and
thoroughly at home in the wilderness. In *The Last of the Mohicans* and

ever since, Americans have depicted the Seven Years' War as a kind of dress rehearsal for the American Revolution, the time when colonists felt their first stirrings of independence as they fought to wrestle the continent from their native enemies and recognized the weaknesses of their own imperial overlords.

Fenimore Cooper was a novelist, not a historian, and he was writing fifty years after the Declaration of Independence, when it was easy to connect the dots between the Fort William Henry Massacre and the creation of a new nation twenty years later. No one at the time of the Seven Years' War described it as a first step toward American independence, however, and in many ways it strengthened rather than loosened the bonds of empire that tied the colonies to Great Britain. A different story unfolds when we examine the war from the perspective of its participants, native and colonial, British and French, soldiers and civilians, men and women. The Seven Years' War had a transformative impact on colonial America. It brought professional European armies and large-scale military operations to North America, and it engulfed colonial and Native American peoples in unprecedented levels of violence. Through the construction of forts and military roads, it opened the trans-Appalachian frontier to invasion by European settlers and soldiers, setting off a conflict with the native inhabitants of that region that would not end for sixty years. For many of its participants, the war was a spiritual as well as a military struggle. French Catholics and British Protestants demonized each other as corrupters of Christianity, and among several Indian nations, the war inspired movements aimed at restoring Native American power by reviving traditional spiritual customs and beliefs. The war also transformed the map of North America, leaving the British Empire in control of the continent east of the Mississippi River and erasing the French claims to Canada and Louisiana. This is a story more complicated and more interesting than that told in *The Last of the Mohicans*, and it is best understood by hearing from the full range of people involved.

WHAT'S IN A NAME?

Part of the problem with modern Americans' misunderstandings about the Seven Years' War is that people have never quite agreed on what to call it. To the generation who fought the American Revolution, it was the Old French War, but that did not distinguish it from a number of Anglo-French wars in North America between 1689 and 1760. French

Canadians call it *La Guerre de la Conquête* (the War of Conquest), but it is known more commonly in North America today as the French and Indian War. In European history books, the conflict is known as the Seven Years' War, an unimaginative name derived from the British and French declarations of war in 1756 and the Treaty of Paris in 1763. In North America, however, the war started with a skirmish in the Ohio country in 1754 and ended in 1760, with the fall of Canada. Thus, in American history books, the duration of the war never quite aligns with what is implied by its name. Lawrence Henry Gipson, who devoted his professional life to writing the fifteen-volume *The British Empire before the American Revolution* (1936–1970), called the conflict the Great War for Empire. Gipson and historians of his generation lived through World War II, and they recognized that the conflict between Britain and France in the 1750s had similar global dimensions and in fact might have justifiably been called the first world war. Today, as a new generation of historians have embraced the field of Atlantic history, they have returned to writing about the war's global impact in international trade, spread of disease, and human migration.

Despite Gipson's efforts, "Seven Years' War" and "French and Indian War" remain the most commonly used names for the conflict. Both will yield results in bibliographic searches, but with subtle differences between them. Historians who want to put the war in a global, or at least an Atlantic, context prefer to describe it as the Seven Years' War. Those more interested in its impact on the British North American colonies and their road to independence are more inclined to call it the French and Indian War. The title of this book, *The Seven Years' War in North America*, reflects a desire to have it both ways, to embrace different perspectives in the source selections but also to keep the focus on northern North America, where the war originated and had its most important impact for colonists and Native Americans.

THE FRENCH AND BRITISH EMPIRES IN NORTH AMERICA

In 1688, Parliament chased the Catholic monarch James II off the British throne and replaced him with William of Orange, a Dutch prince who was married to James's Protestant daughter Mary. The accession of William and Mary to the throne ensured that the line of succession would remain with James's Protestant heirs, a tremendous relief to Parliament and the Church of England. It also drew England into William's wars against Louis XIV, king of France and Europe's most powerful monarch, and it intensified the religious tensions between Protestant Britain and Catholic France. This disruption in Britain's dynastic politics initiated a series of Anglo-French wars that would involve other European powers, overseas colonies, and theaters of conflict around the globe until the defeat of Napoleon at Waterloo in 1815.

The native and colonial peoples of North America were drawn into these conflicts in a number of ways. Wars waged among Europe's imperial powers gave people living in their colonial possessions license to wage wars of opportunity against each other as well. In the name of distant monarchs, French and British colonists raided each other's shipping on the high seas and plundered each other's settlements on land. Sometimes colonists were recruited in one part of the empire to go fight in another, such as when British colonists in North America were deployed by the thousands for expeditions against two Spanish strongholds in the Caribbean, Cartagena in 1741 and Havana in 1762. In other instances, European wars affected native and colonial peoples by disrupting transatlantic trade or by creating refugee populations in the Old World, some of whom came to America in search of new homes. In the seventeenth century, the Atlantic Ocean had isolated American colonies from European wars. In the eighteenth century, the Atlantic became a highway for exporting such conflicts abroad.

By 1750, Britain and France were the two most significant imperial powers in eastern North America. The Dutch colony of New Netherland had been conquered by the English in 1664 and renamed New York. Spanish Florida was a military and missionary outpost, isolated from the rest of Spain's New World empire. But New France and British North America developed differently, turning what had been uncertain toeholds of settlement in the seventeenth century into solid foundations of imperial power in the eighteenth.

French power in North America emanated from the St. Lawrence River valley, which connected the North Atlantic with the Great Lakes. French *habitants* worked farms along the banks of the St. Lawrence and in the province of Acadia (modern Nova Scotia), making the best of Canada's short growing season, but the lifeblood of New France's economy was the fur trade, which extended along interior waterways as far west as the Missouri River. While French fur traders took Indian wives and forged kin relations with their customers, French missionaries immersed themselves in native languages and cultures so they could save Indian souls. Although their numbers were small, the French profoundly affected the lives of the Indians they encountered. The fur trade upset traditional economies, new diseases ravaged native populations, and missionary work caused divisions between Indians who converted to Christianity and those who rejected it. The impact of these changes was evident in the *reserves* of the St. Lawrence Valley, where Indians from different nations, converts and traditionalists alike, mixed with one another and occasionally their colonial neighbors. At the start of the eighteenth century, the French established the colony of Louisiana at the mouth of the Mississippi River, another important point of entry into the continent. As was the case in Canada, the colonial population of Louisiana grew fitfully. In an effort to enforce religious orthodoxy abroad as well as at home, the French crown prohibited non-Catholics from emigrating to its colonies, and those French who did venture across the Atlantic preferred the sugar islands of the Caribbean to North America. Nevertheless, the southern deerskin trade supported the French presence along the Gulf coast. By 1750, the combined colonial population of Canada and Louisiana was only about 55,000 people, but the geographic reach of the French in North America was truly impressive. Despite the much larger number of British colonists there, British observers believed that the French held the strategic advantage because they had managed to extend their trade and influence so far into the continent's interior.

In contrast, Britain's North American colonies hugged the eastern seaboard and pushed unevenly westward toward the Appalachian Mountains (see Map 1). Fourteen mainland colonies from Nova Scotia to Georgia had been founded at different times by different people and possessed different types of governments. In the Chesapeake Bay and southward, a plantation economy built on African slavery and cash crops emerged. North of the Chesapeake, the economy was more diversified, ranging from fur trading and fishing in coastal New England to mixed agriculture and livestock breeding in the Delaware and Hudson valleys. With the exception of Dutch New Netherland, the founding populations of these colonies had been overwhelmingly English in origin, but after 1680 new waves of migration gave them a heterogeneous character. Scots-Irish, the descendants of Scottish colonizers of northern Ireland, poured into the mid-Atlantic colonies, as did German-speaking peoples from the Rhine River valley and French-speaking Protestants who had been denied religious freedom in their homelands but who also were excluded from French colonies abroad. Africans carried against their will into the Atlantic slave trade likewise changed the demographic makeup of British North America, especially in the South. The British government encouraged foreign Protestants to populate its American colonies and eased their naturalization as British subjects. Even non-Protestant groups, such as Catholics and Jews, found tacit toleration in some parts of British North America because no single ethnic or religious group possessed the power to exclude them.

This rapid and heterogeneous population growth distinguished British North America from other colonial regions in the New World. Europeans and Africans found the temperate climate of the eastern seaboard healthier than the Caribbean, and they achieved positive rates of natural reproduction there more quickly than anywhere else in the Americas. In 1751, Benjamin Franklin estimated that one million British subjects were living in North America and that they were doubling every twenty-five years. He celebrated how this growth would add to British wealth and world power, so long as there was enough land in the colonies to sustain it.

Franklin's analysis placed the North American colonies at the center of the British Empire's future. The War of the Austrian Succession (known in British North America as King George's War) ended in 1748 with no clear resolution of Britain's and France's competing claims to the continent. Both sides claimed the eastern Great Lakes and knew that they provided the best route for connecting the continent's interior to the northern Atlantic seaboard. Both especially coveted the Ohio country, which connected Lake Erie to the Mississippi Valley by way of the Ohio River. Whichever side succeeded in asserting possession of the Ohio country would secure a corridor for colonizing the modern states of Ohio, Kentucky, Michigan, Indiana, and Illinois and monopolize its potentially profitable fur trade. Although removed by hundreds of miles of wilderness from the nearest colonial seat of government, the Ohio country held the key to the continent (Documents 1–6).

NATIVE AMERICAN CONFEDERACIES

While the French and British were building their empires in North America, changes were also under way for the continent's indigenous peoples. Colonization in the seventeenth century had brought a shock wave of disease and warfare to coastal Indians, uprooting them or confining them to shrinking land bases surrounded by hostile neighbors. Those who lived farther away from colonial populations fared better, especially if they controlled the land and waterways that led to the interior. By the early eighteenth century, such Indians were forging new political alliances by taking other native groups into their orbit and using their numbers to augment their own power. Along the southern ranges of the Appalachian Mountains, the Creek and Cherokee confederacies emerged as native power brokers in the deerskin trade. The Creeks took advantage of their position between French traders along the Gulf coast and British traders in Georgia to extract favorable prices and diplomatic presents from both sides. The Cherokees did the same with the governments of Virginia and South Carolina and French traders based on the Alabama River. Power was local and widely dispersed in these native confederacies. Neither the Creeks nor the Cherokees possessed a centralized government that could compel other Indians to do as they pleased, but bonds of kinship and shared interests encouraged these groups to act cooperatively when dealing with outsiders.

The Iroquois were the most powerful Indian confederacy in the North. The original five nations of the confederacy—from east to west, the Mohawks, Oneidas, Onondagas, Cayugas, and Senecas—inhabited the region south of Lake Ontario between French Canada and British New York (see Map 1). In treaties negotiated in Montreal and Albany in 1701, the Iroquois established neutrality with the French and British, enabling them to continue trading and conducting diplomacy with both sides. The British colonies referred to their alliance with the Iroquois as the Covenant Chain, and they liked to describe it as an exclusive relationship that bound the Iroquois in submission to the British crown in exchange for its protection. The Iroquois, however, continued to conduct diplomacy independently with the governor-general of New France, whom they called Onontio, "the Great Father." The Iroquois also expanded their influence by allowing Indians displaced from other regions to settle in their territory as "props" of their confederacy. The Tuscaroras, who migrated northward from the Carolinas during the 1710s, became the "sixth nation" of the Iroquois confederacy, but numerous smaller groups—Mahicans, Conestogas, Conoys, Tutelos, Nanticokes, and others—followed a similar strategy to survival, finding refuge from dispossession by migrating into Iroquois territory.

By 1750 another important confederacy had emerged. The region known as the Forks of the Ohio, where the Allegheny and Monongahela rivers meet to form the Ohio River (modern Pittsburgh), attracted Indian migrants because of its plentiful game and rich soil. Delawares and Shawnees from eastern Pennsylvania and Senecas from the Niagara region mixed with one another in the towns they established there. The Iroquois confederacy claimed that the Ohio country and these Indians were under its authority. Although a strong cultural and familial kinship existed among many of the Iroquois and Ohio Indians, distance and the dispersed nature of native political power meant that the Ohio Indians acted independently in promoting their own interests and security. They valued trade with the British and the French, but in treaty conferences with both they were plainspoken about their desire to keep European settlers out of their country.

THE ORIGINS OF THE SEVEN YEARS' WAR

French fur traders reached Indians in the Ohio country by way of Niagara and Detroit, forts built on the passages between Lakes Ontario and Erie and between Lakes Erie and Huron, respectively. The French had older commercial ties to the Ohio Indians than did the British, but Canada's long winters made their supply of goods expensive and unreliable. British traders reached the Ohio country by traveling overland through Virginia and Pennsylvania, providing more plentiful goods at cheaper prices. In 1749, the governor-general of New France sent a military expedition into the Ohio country to expel British traders and assert French possession of the region. The Ohio Indians did not welcome this show of force and resented the insults shown to their British trading partners (Document 1). Despite these objections, the French grew more forceful and began fortifying the route between Lake Erie and the Forks of the Ohio.

British colonists watched the French progress in the Ohio country with trepidation. During the 1740s, the Pennsylvania government initiated diplomatic relations with the Ohio Indians, but it failed to supply those Indians with requested military aid against the French. Since Pennsylvania's founding by Quaker William Penn, the Quaker principle of pacifism had figured prominently in the colony's Indian relations. Also, by the 1750s the colony's assembly was at an impasse with the Penn family over who would fund appropriations necessary for the colony's defense. While the Pennsylvanians lingered in political gridlock, a group of land speculators in Virginia formed the Ohio Company, intending to secure the Forks of the Ohio for themselves. Under pretense of engaging in the fur trade, the Ohio Company sent workmen there in early 1754 to build a fort. Within a few weeks they were booted out by a larger French force, which then built Fort Duquesne on the site.

Virginia governor Robert Dinwiddie had strict orders from his London superiors to defend British territory from French encroachments but not to provoke war. In late 1753, he sent twenty-one-year-old militia officer George Washington to tell the French in the Ohio country that they were trespassing. The French responded by telling Washington that he was trespassing on French territory (Document 7). After learning that the French had occupied the Forks of the Ohio, Dinwiddie sent Washington back to the region, this time with two hundred militiamen. Washington was prepared to use force to remove the French, but he stumbled badly. In a surprise attack on a French scouting party, the Virginians wounded a French officer who claimed to be on a diplomatic mission from Fort Duquesne. An Indian in Washington's party finished off the dying Frenchman with a tomahawk blow to the skull, ending any chance for a diplomatic solution to the crisis (Document 8). Realizing he was outnumbered by the French at Fort Duquesne, Washington retreated to a hastily constructed stockade he named Fort Necessity, where after a dispiriting engagement he surrendered to the French on July 4, 1754 (Document 9).

The cold war in the Ohio country had turned hot. Unlike previous imperial wars that started in Europe and spilled over into the Americas, the Seven Years' War broke out on a distant fringe of European empire, in a place few European ministers of state could have pointed to on a map. The disastrous performance of Washington's force at Fort Necessity convinced British observers that the colonies were too divided to cooperate effectively in answering the French threat. One month before the surrender of Fort Necessity, Benjamin Franklin had published the first political cartoon in American history. Labeled "Join, or Die," the cartoon featured a snake cut into several pieces, representing the colonies from Massachusetts to South Carolina. A few weeks later, he proposed a plan of intercolonial union at the Albany Congress, a treaty conference convened to renew the Covenant Chain alliance with the Iroquois. Although the colonial assemblies rejected the Albany Plan, the king's ministers in London did take one significant step toward American union. They appointed General Edward Braddock the commander in chief of British forces in North America and sent him across the Atlantic with two regiments of regular troops to accomplish what the Virginians had failed to do: turn the French out of the Ohio country.

In 1755, Braddock launched an ambitious, multipronged plan. He would lead his regular and provincial troops on a march from the upper Potomac River to Fort Duquesne at the Forks of the Ohio, cutting a road through the wilderness wide enough to accommodate his supply train and artillery. In the meantime, Governor William Shirley of Massachusetts would recruit an army of provincial soldiers to attack the French at Niagara, and New York Indian agent William Johnson would lead another army of colonial and native recruits against Fort

Saint-Frédéric, a French post on Lake Champlain. Each campaign could be construed as a defensive measure to remove French encroachments on British territory, a necessary diplomatic cover because war had not yet been declared in Europe. For colonists and Indians, however, there was no mistaking that Braddock's arrival had turned a new page in American warfare: He led the largest deployment of redcoats ever sent to America, and it was accompanied by all the auxiliaries of a modern European army, including an artillery train, civilian laborers and female camp followers, and a military hospital (Document 15). His road to Fort Duquesne would be a major project of military engineering, and colonial troops were going to be mobilized on an unprecedented scale for the king's service.

Some Ohio Indians exhibited an interest in assisting the expedition against Fort Duquesne, but Braddock alienated them at the outset by declaring that "no Savage Should Inherit the Land" after the French were removed (Document 11). As a result, most Indians in the region either stood aside as Braddock marched toward the Forks or threw their lot in with the French, who supplied them generously. On July 9, 1755, as Braddock's army moved within ten miles of its objective, a combined French and Indian force from Fort Duquesne tore it to pieces, taking advantage of the cover provided by the surrounding forest to pour fire into the confused British troops (Document 10). Braddock received a mortal wound; his aide-de-camp George Washington managed to survive but witnessed the second crushing defeat of the British in the Ohio country in a year's time.

In New York, Shirley's and Johnson's campaigns stalled. The two men competed against each other for Indian allies among the Iroquois. Johnson, who lived in the Mohawk Valley and was renowned for his influence among his Indian neighbors, convinced many Mohawks to join him, but warriors from the other Iroquois nations stayed home, unimpressed by the British mobilization. Shirley's army proceeded no farther west than Oswego, the British fur-trading post on the southeastern shore of Lake Ontario. Johnson devoted his energies to defensive measures, building Fort William Henry to protect the passage from Lake George to Albany. On September 8, 1755, his forces unexpectedly engaged a French army moving south from Lake Champlain led by Jean-Armand, baron de Dieskau. Many of Johnson's Mohawk allies, including the pro-British chief King Hendrick, were killed. The casualties on both sides were about equal, but Dieskau's army withdrew first, allowing Johnson to claim victory. The Mohawks' losses, however, made the Iroquois even more reluctant to join the British cause.

Also in 1755, the British moved preemptively against the French in Nova Scotia. The borders between British Nova Scotia and French Canada were unclear, but the political sympathies of the region's population were obvious. It consisted of fifteen thousand French-speaking Acadians, descendants of farmers and fishermen who settled there in the seventeenth century. To protect their lives and property, the Acadians swore neutrality in Anglo-French wars, but the British distrusted their Catholic faith and suspected them of aiding Abenaki and Micmac Indians in their raids along the New England frontier. British troops captured two French forts in this contested borderland and then began forcibly deporting the Acadians. This uprooting became a diaspora that carried the Acadians across the Atlantic, into the Caribbean, and to other mainland North American colonies. It also foreshadowed the other extreme measures the British would take against perceived civilian and Native American enemies during the Seven Years' War.

THE FRENCH ASCENDANT, 1756–1757

In early 1756, Britain and France declared war against each other, transforming the hostilities in North America into a global conflict. In the war's European theater, France, Austria, Russia, and Sweden allied against Britain, Prussia, and several German principalities ruled by the British king George II, whose German-speaking father had ascended to the British throne at Parliament's invitation in 1714. Britain and France also moved against each other's colonies in the Caribbean, Africa, and India, preying on each other's trade in spices, slaves, and sugar. Although the war had started in North America, protecting these far-flung interests made it impossible for either Britain or France to concentrate its military resources entirely there once war was declared.

For Britain's rulers, the strategy for fighting the war in North America seemed obvious: exploit the enormous advantages the British colonies enjoyed over New France in population and wealth. The new commander in chief appointed after Braddock's death, Scottish general John Campbell, the Earl of Loudoun, arrived in America in 1756 and immediately began requisitioning men and supplies from the colonial assemblies. The assemblies responded with little enthusiasm, waiting for other colonies to make their contributions first and placing conditions on how troops and matériel paid for with their funding could be deployed. Loudoun had little patience for such legislative foot-dragging and even less respect for the quality of the provincial troops raised by the assemblies. He preferred to recruit colonial Americans directly into the British army, where they could be subjected to regular army training and discipline and the assemblies could not interfere with their use. But colonial recruits preferred the shorter enlistments, easier discipline, and better pay of provincial forces. Colonists also bristled at the command structure imposed by Braddock and Loudoun in America, in which regular British army officers at the rank of captain or above outranked all Americans holding officer commissions from colonial governments regardless of their rank or seniority in service. Colonial officers regarded this rule as an insult to their honor, and some resigned their commissions rather than endure this second-class status while serving with British forces.

While Loudoun grew frustrated with his inability to corral the assemblies and make reliable troops out of colonial Americans, the French military establishment in Canada experienced its own transformation. Since the seventeenth century, the French had relied on an intercultural blending of forces to defend Canada from its enemies. Like their British counterparts, French colonists were compelled to engage in militia service, but the French crown also maintained *troupes de la marine* in Canada, professional soldiers recruited in Europe but led by Canadian officers with close ties to Native Americans. Indian warriors, mostly drawn from the *reserves* around Quebec and Montreal, also served with the French soldiers and militia, although they had to be constantly courted with diplomatic presents to do so. During the late seventeenth century, the failure of French armies to conquer the Iroquois had taught them hard lessons about fighting in the North American environment. Following the lead of their Indian allies, they learned the methods of *la petite guerre*, an irregular, guerrilla-style warfare that relied on the rapid movement of small parties unencumbered by supply trains or artillery (Documents 13 and 14). During the Anglo-French wars of 1689 to 1748, French and Indian war parties from Canada repeatedly raided frontier settlements in New England and New York, carrying away hundreds of captives and thwarting efforts by the British to secure their possession of these borderlands.

In the spring of 1756, General Louis-Joseph, marquis de Montcalm, arrived in Canada with one thousand French regulars. A professional soldier trained in European methods of warfare, Montcalm focused his war plan on reducing British forts rather than raiding frontier civilians. He had his first success at Oswego, the British post on Lake Ontario that Shirley's army had spent the previous campaign season strengthening. It fell quickly to Montcalm's troops in August 1756. The following year, Montcalm occupied Fort Carillon at Ticonderoga, a strategic passage between Lake Champlain and Lake George, and then used it as a base for launching his siege of Fort William Henry. In 1758, he held firm at Fort Carillon and repelled a much larger British force from Albany (Document 16). With resources much more limited than those of his enemy, Montcalm was succeeding where Braddock and Loudoun had failed: He was waging a European-style war in the American wilderness.

While Montcalm delivered serial humiliations to the British forces in New York, a different kind of war raged along the mid-Atlantic frontier. After Braddock's defeat in July 1755, the surviving portion of his army retreated eastward, leaving the colonial backcountry dangerously exposed. During the following fall, French and Indian war parties out of Fort Duquesne raided frontier homesteads and communities in a broad arc from the Lehigh Valley in northeastern Pennsylvania to Virginia's Shenandoah Valley. The carnage was particularly shocking in Pennsylvania, which up to that point had never warred with its Indian neighbors and had no militia to call out in response to the raids or fortifications to protect its frontier inhabitants. Newspaper accounts described these raids as arbitrary and unwarranted, but the Indians who conducted them were targeting settlers and squatters on land they believed had been sold out from under them in deals conducted by the Iroquois during the 1740s and 1750s. Their grievances were legitimate. The Iroquois had managed to preserve their homelands by selling land elsewhere in Pennsylvania, Maryland, and Virginia. Delawares, Shawnees, and others who had already endured dispossession in eastern Pennsylvania were now adamant in their refusal to sell or cede territory in the Ohio country.

For many colonists, frontier warfare meant enduring captivity among the enemy. The captivity experience challenged traditional gender roles: Male captives were rendered powerless and suffered humiliations and torments such as being stripped naked in front of their families and neighbors and ritually tortured. Women and children, by contrast, were likely to be adopted into Indian families who treated them with tenderness and care. Captivity narratives written by men and women exhibited a range of reactions to Indian culture, from horror to grudging admiration to deep emotional attachment (Documents 18–20). In peace negotiations, the British insisted on the return of all captives. This policy shocked some observers when they witnessed the forced return to colonial society of captives who did not wish to leave their adoptive families (Document 21).

The frontier war in the mid-Atlantic exposed the tensions underlying the religious and ethnic diversity of British North America. Scots-Irish and German backcountry settlers, many of them squatters on land claimed by the Penn family or planter-speculators such as George Washington, formed their own militias to retaliate against the Indians, paying little heed to their colonial governments and taking little care to distinguish between Indians the British considered friendly or hostile. Adopting the same tactics that Indian war parties were using against them, they killed noncombatants, burned Indian homes and crops, and scalped the dead so that they could be paid bounties offered by colonial governments. In Virginia, Governor Dinwiddie recruited Indians from farther south to fight against the French-allied Ohio Indians, but the Cherokees tired of the slow progress of British arms and abandoned them in 1758. In Pennsylvania, Indians living in the Susquehanna Valley exhibited more solidarity with their kin in the Ohio country than with their colonial neighbors to the east.

THE BRITISH ASCENDANT, 1758–1760

Despite the ineptitude exhibited by British forces at the war's outset, they still possessed undeniable advantages over the French in North America. William Pitt, who became prime minister of Britain in late 1756, knew this and began diverting more of Britain's military resources to the colonies while paying Prussia subsidies to fight the war in Europe. To gain the Americans' cooperation, Pitt promised the assemblies that they would be reimbursed for their wartime appropriations, and he instituted new rules regarding military rank that made American officers in provincial commands the equals of their peers among the regulars. These changes convinced the colonial assemblies to open their checkbooks and reinvigorated the recruitment of Americans into provincial forces. Pitt also increased the number of redcoats in America. Approximately eighteen thousand served there during the campaigns of 1758, a number that would not be equaled until the American Revolution.

As Pitt and the colonial assemblies were marshaling Britain's resources in America, the French were coming up against the limits of theirs. Bad harvests and a British naval blockade made it difficult for France to supply its North American forces. Indian allies remained loyal only so long as the French "Great Father," Onontio, honored the terms of the alliance by providing them with presents, trade, and weapons and ammunition (Document 22). After the Fort William Henry campaign, the warriors from the *pays d'en haut* went home disenchanted with Montcalm and his method of warfare and did not return to the French cause. Despite his successes at Oswego and Fort William Henry, Montcalm found himself on the defensive in 1758.

Pitt made General Jeffery Amherst his new commander in chief in America and placed him in charge of an amphibious assault on Louisbourg, the French fortress that guarded the mouth of the St. Lawrence River. Along with his second-in-command, General James Wolfe, Amherst executed a successful siege that lasted seven weeks, relying on a force made up almost entirely of British redcoats and sailors. Meanwhile, General John Forbes assembled an army of regular and provincial troops to march on Fort Duquesne. Rather than using Braddock's Road, Forbes opted to cut a new route west from Carlisle, Pennsylvania. This decision alienated Virginians, who knew that the new road would strengthen Pennsylvania's claim to the Ohio country, but Forbes persevered, taking care to fortify the route at regular intervals so as to avoid the sort of all-out retreat that had doomed Braddock's army. His campaign was aided by timely diplomacy conducted by missionary Christian Frederick Post and Delaware chief Pisquetomen, who carried peace overtures between the Ohio Indians and the Pennsylvanians (Document 23). At a treaty conference in Easton, Pennsylvania, in October 1758, the British agreed to restore some of the disputed land sold by the Iroquois and to withdraw from the Ohio country after expelling the French. These concessions convinced the Ohio Indians to stand aside as Forbes made his last push toward the Forks of the Ohio. The French commander at Fort Duquesne, realizing his situation was untenable, blew up the fort and retreated toward Lake Erie. Forbes had exorcised the ghost of Braddock.

In 1759, British forces continued their assault on New France. The previous year, Lieutenant Colonel John Bradstreet had led a small army of provincial troops in taking Fort Frontenac, the French post that guarded the passage from Lake Ontario to the St. Lawrence River. Without Frontenac, the French could not supply their troops and Indian allies along the Great Lakes, and the British were able to reoccupy Oswego. Fort Niagara was now dangerously exposed, and General John Prideaux assembled an army to march against it. Sir William Johnson (having been knighted for his victory at Lake George four years earlier) served as his second-in-command and recruited nearly one thousand Iroquois warriors to join the expedition. Prideaux was killed by an errant shell from his own artillery, but Johnson took over and completed a siege that ended with a French surrender in late July (Document 12). As Prideaux and Johnson were reducing Fort Niagara, Amherst led another army north from Albany into the Champlain Valley. His advance forced the undersupplied French garrisons at Fort Carillon and Fort Saint-Frédéric to blow up their posts and retreat toward Montreal. A few months later, the New England scout Robert Rogers led a raid that destroyed the Abenaki town of Saint-François, one of the *reserves* that had helped to defend Canada.

The most stunning British victory in 1759 came when Amherst's protégé James Wolfe led nine thousand regulars and a fleet of warships up the St. Lawrence River from Louisbourg for an amphibious assault on Quebec, the capital of New France. Wolfe's fleet arrived within range of the city in July, but then several weeks of maneuvering followed as he tried to find a landing place for his troops and Montcalm prepared to defend Quebec. On the night of September 12, Wolfe's troops scaled a cliff from their river landing to the Plains of Abraham, high ground that commanded the city. At dawn, Montcalm assembled his forces to meet Wolfe's, rushing into battle without adequate reinforcements. Both commanders received mortal wounds in the battle, but the British prevailed. The heart of New France was theirs (Documents 31 and 32). In the denouement of the war's North American operations, Amherst oversaw an operation the following summer that had three British armies converge on Montreal, the last French stronghold in Canada. In the face of this overwhelming force, the city surrendered. New France was now in British hands.

UNCERTAIN VICTORY, 1761–1763

On both sides of the Atlantic, the British celebrated the fall of Canada as an epochal event. In New England, ministers preached sermons of thanksgiving for deliverance from their Catholic enemy, and colonial land speculators and fur traders anticipated great profits to be reaped from undisputed possession of the Ohio country. Some London commentators argued that Canada should be returned to France in exchange for one of its sugar colonies in the Caribbean, but that idea aroused opposition from William Pitt, Benjamin Franklin, and other critics who believed that Britain's ascendancy in North America would give it an edge against France around the globe (Documents 33 and 34). When Spain entered the war as an ally of France, Pitt saw an opportunity to extend his successful strategy against another rival empire, but he resigned his office when the king hesitated to follow. Nevertheless, in 1762 Britain moved against Spain and won two more stunning victories, taking Havana, Cuba, and Manila in the Philippines.

Britain used these conquests to reshape the map of North America in the Peace of Paris, signed in early 1763. France surrendered all of its possessions in North America east of the Mississippi to the British, except for New Orleans, which went to the Spanish, as did the vast Louisiana territory west of the Mississippi. In exchange for the return of Havana, the Spanish surrendered Florida to the British. Britain restored some but not all of the Caribbean islands it had seized from the French and kept conquests it had won in India. The British also restored Manila to the Spanish and Gorée, a West African trading post, to the French. As was typical with the treaties that ended eighteenth-century wars, European diplomats were concerned with restoring the balance of power at home and overseas, but the impact of the Peace of Paris on the British Empire was unmistakable. It was now the unrivaled power in North America and the Indian subcontinent. Colonies that had started as privately funded commercial enterprises had become continental dominions whose populations had the potential to dwarf the number of the king's subjects living in the British Isles.

That assumption of power did not go unchallenged among the native peoples of North America. In 1759, as Wolfe and Amherst were bringing New France to its knees, war broke out between the Cherokees and the colonies of South Carolina and Virginia. Amherst dispatched regular troops to the region to conduct scorched-earth campaigns against Cherokee towns in 1760 and 1761 (Document 24). In the *pays d'en haut*, Indians formerly allied with the French became restive as British troops occupied French forts. William Johnson, who served as the crown's superintendent of Indian affairs, tried to calm them at a treaty conference in Detroit in 1761, promising redress for their grievances and admitting them into the Covenant Chain alliance (Document 25), but Amherst was not interested in stepping into the shoes of the French "Great Father." During the war, he had grudgingly authorized Johnson's expenses in Indian diplomacy, realizing that the only thing more expensive than keeping Indian allies was not having them at all. But with New France conquered, he ordered Johnson to cease distributing diplomatic presents and to curtail the amount of gunpowder made available to Indians. They complained bitterly about these measures, which they interpreted as an effort by the British to reduce them to economic slavery and seize their land.

In 1763, Indians throughout the *pays d'en haut* took up arms. In surprise raids, they killed or captured the small garrisons of British soldiers stationed throughout the Great Lakes and Ohio country and laid siege to the three largest western British forts: Niagara, Detroit, and Pitt (built on the site of Fort Duquesne). They also renewed their raids on colonial settlements that encroached on their land, taking hundreds of captives and terrorizing the mid-Atlantic frontier. The British blamed this uprising on the Ottawa war chief Pontiac, who led the attack on Detroit and helped spread the message of a Delaware prophet who encouraged Indians to reject Christianity, revive their old ways, and live apart from whites (Document 35). The geographic extent and violent intensity of Pontiac's War, however, indicated that it arose more from shared grievances inspired by Amherst's policies than the spiritual vision or political acumen of any one man.

Pontiac's War also marked intensified violence in the methods and language British officers and American colonists used to fight Indians. Writing to one of his subordinate officers about the siege of Fort Pitt, Amherst referred to Indians as "this Execrable Race" and discussed the possibility of using smallpox as a weapon against them (Document 28). In Lancaster County, Pennsylvania, a group of frontier vigilantes known as the Paxton Boys murdered an unarmed group of twenty Indian men, women, and children in retaliation for raids in which they had played no part. The savagery of this crime shocked many colonists, but the Paxton Boys defended their actions by describing all Indians as inherently treacherous (Documents 29 and 30).

Without aid from the French, the Indians of the *pays d'en haut* lacked the support necessary to sustain Pontiac's War. As the construction of Fort Pitt made clear, the British army was in their territory to stay. Johnson told the Indians that the redcoats were there for their benefit, to regulate the fur trade and to keep settlers off their land, but the presence of the British army encouraged exactly what it sought to prevent. Military roads opened Indian territory to squatters and unlicensed traders. The garrisons kept at places such as Forts Pitt and Detroit became magnets for civilians, who planted towns outside their walls and relied on their troops for security. In an effort to restore order in its newly conquered American territory, the British crown issued a proclamation in October 1763 imposing a boundary line between colonial and Indian land that ran along the Appalachian Mountains (see Map 1, page 2). Colonists were prohibited from settling west of the line until royal agents negotiated land sales from the native owners. The Proclamation of 1763 displeased colonial elites who had invested in speculative land ventures, and it was generally ignored by squatters, but it committed the British government to keeping several thousand redcoats in North America to police a vast and potentially hostile frontier. Empire had its price.

LEGACIES OF THE SEVEN YEARS' WAR IN NORTH AMERICA

Historians have long debated the causal relationship between the Seven Years' War and the American Revolution. The conquest of Canada created a host of unforeseen problems for the British in North America that they would struggle to solve right up until shots were fired at Lexington and Concord in April 1775. Fighting the war had doubled Britain's national debt and placed the king's subjects at home under an enormous tax burden. For the first time, the crown had to maintain a peacetime army in North America. It also had to figure out a way to govern the former French subjects in Canada and Louisiana and the former Spanish subjects in Florida, while at the same time regulating the fur trade and western land sales in a way that would keep the Indians of the trans-Appalachian West at peace. In 1754, the North American colonies had been situated on a distant fringe of the crown's dominions, an afterthought to most British policymakers compared to India, the Caribbean, or Ireland. After 1763, North America loomed larger than any of those places on the "to do" lists of the ministry and Parliament.

The decisions made by British officials as they grappled with the problems of victory and the reactions of colonists and Indians to those decisions were profoundly influenced by their wartime experiences. Each of these groups would have told a different story about the origins, progress, and outcomes of the war, which is why it is so important to appreciate the multiple perspectives depicted in the source selections that follow. War is a destructive enterprise, but it is also an educational one. British officers and soldiers adapted to a new environment; American colonists had their first significant encounters with royal power in generations; Native Americans forged new strategies for uniting in resistance to European expansion. Out of these differing experiences grew different visions for the future of North America and its native and colonial inhabitants.

Like distant cousins reunited after years of separation, Britons and colonial Americans learned much about each other in the Seven Years' War. British military and government officials realized the enormous wealth and potential that North America possessed. Some officers and soldiers liked North America so much that they settled there. The material prosperity of colonial Americans was evident in their physical health, diet, clothes, and housing. They also enjoyed lower taxes and greater religious freedom than their British contemporaries. In light of the meagerness of life for Britain's working poor, North America deserved its reputation as a place where laboring men and women could prosper and pass that same economic security on to their children. But colonial Americans also seemed a bit spoiled from the British perspective. They made poor soldiers because they lacked discipline and respect for their superiors. Their governments were jealously protective of their presumed powers and unwilling to shoulder their share of the common defense. If colonies were like children, then these needed to learn proper subjection to parental authority, and they could certainly afford a few small taxes to pay for the war that had won a continent for them.

Colonial Americans had formed some distinct impressions of their British counterparts as well. On the one hand, they reveled in the contributions they had made to Britain's imperial ascent. They had expended their blood and treasure in campaigns fought in the Ohio country, Great Lakes, Canada, and the Caribbean. They had faced the trials of European-style warfare bravely—Washington survived Braddock's defeat, and Johnson led the victories at Lake George and Niagara—and they had taught British regulars a thing or two about frontier warfare. Robert Rogers, the New Englander who had led the raid that destroyed Saint-François in 1759, was hailed as the great American Indian fighter when he visited London in the 1760s (Document 17). The colonists believed they had proved their worth to Britain, not just as producers or consumers of goods but as fellow subjects who helped defeat Britain's Catholic enemies and deserved to share in the rewards of victory. Certainly, the crown and Parliament realized the extent of their sacrifices and would not presume to impose on their rights as free men.

For Native Americans, the Seven Years' War ended with a different kind of reckoning. The fall of New France made it impossible for native confederacies such as the Iroquois and Cherokees to play European powers off against each another as they had in the past. Indians now depended entirely on Britain for the material goods they acquired in the fur trade, and the diplomacy conducted by Johnson and other royal agents became more exploitive, shifting away from mediating differences to acquiring Indian land. In 1768, Johnson concluded the Treaty of Fort Stanwix with the Iroquois, plying them with cash and goods for land cessions that pushed the boundary line farther west. These cessions ignited another wave of land-grabbing and frontier hostilities that eventually blended into the frontier warfare of the American Revolution. The Seven Years' War also seemed to intensify racial divisions between colonists and Indians. Voices on both sides of the cultural divide grew more insistent on the need to live apart and pursue "separate paths." The anti-Indian rhetoric used in colonial newspapers and pamphlets became strident and inflammatory, condemning all Indians as inherently treacherous and condoning preemptive violence against them.

The Seven Years' War did not cause the American Revolution, but it did reshape the cultural geography of North America in a way that affected generations to come. The interior of the continent would be colonized by English-speaking people planting laws, governments, and institutions inspired by British models. The British conquerors of Canada did not attempt to eradicate its French heritage. They granted toleration to Roman Catholics and allowed the continued use of the French language and French civil law. These concessions were formalized in the Quebec Act of 1774, which restored civilian government to the province. However, French cultural supremacy in Canada would be diluted by British migration to Nova Scotia and Ontario during the eighteenth and nineteenth centuries. Native peoples from the Great Lakes to Florida would likewise feel the pressures of Britain's expanding imperial power, falling into greater dependence on the fur trade and facing pressure to ally with the crown against the colonists in the American Revolution and the War of 1812. Native peoples and colonial Americans alike found their lives intertwined with the fate of the British Empire in North America after 1763 in ways that few could have imagined a decade earlier.

NOTES

[1] There were seven *reserves* in the St. Lawrence Valley that were home to mixed populations of Iroquois, Huron, Abenaki, Algonquin, and other Indians. French missionaries worked in these communities, but not all residents of *reserves* were Christians. Many Indians moved to these communities to be among family and friends or to take advantage of economic opportunities offered by proximity to the French.

[2] Ian K. Steele, *Betrayals: Fort William Henry and the "Massacre"* (New York: Oxford University Press, 1990), 143–44.

PART TWO

The Documents

1

Empires, Indians, and Colonists

The Seven Years' War originated on a colonial borderland, where Indians, colonists, and soldiers engaged in hostilities before any formal declarations of war in Europe. The particular bone of contention among them was the region known as the Ohio country, which encompassed the modern state of Ohio, along with slices of eastern Indiana and western Pennsylvania (see Map 1, page 2). In 1750, it was isolated from French and British populations in North America by the Allegheny Mountains (part of the Appalachians) and the Great Lakes. Its native population included the Miami Indians, as well as migrants from the Delaware, Shawnee, and Iroquois nations. The Ohio country was a vast but remote area, sparsely populated when compared to the eastern seaboard but highly valued by native and European peoples alike.

To the Indians who lived there, the Ohio country was their homeland, and it supplied them with the resources—fertile land and plentiful game—they needed to survive. Many of the Indians who lived along the Allegheny-Ohio watershed were Delawares and Shawnees who had been dispossessed from their previous homes in the river valleys of eastern Pennsylvania. They mixed with Iroquois peoples who migrated south from western New York along the Allegheny River to find better hunting or to escape social and political turmoil associated with the French presence at Niagara. Farther west in the Ohio country, the Miamis had yet to encounter the pressures associated with an expanding colonial population, but they were already deeply involved with the fur trade via French posts along the Great Lakes. Although often grouped together by European observers, the Ohio Indians did not share a single political or ethnic identity. However, as Document 1 makes clear, they had two important bonds: They depended heavily on the fur trade for their material goods, and they did not wish to see their land invaded by European armies or settlers.

French and British colonial officials saw the Ohio country differently. To them, it was the key to possessing the interior of North America because it linked the waterways of the Great Lakes with those of the

Mississippi Valley. Reports from explorers and fur traders confirmed the fertility of this region's soil and its temperate climate. A colony planted in the Ohio country would undoubtedly prosper, first by monopolizing the fur trade with the Indians there and then by cultivating crops and extracting other natural resources for export to overseas markets via the Ohio and Mississippi rivers. The French claimed the Ohio country was theirs by right of discoveries made in the seventeenth century, and they regarded it as a southward extension of Canada. If they secured possession of the Ohio River, they would be able to link their colonial settlements in Canada with those in Louisiana, opening an unbroken corridor for settlement through the heart of the continent. In Document 2, a former governor-general of French Canada explains why he believes that the secret to checking British power in Europe rests in pursuing this colonial plan in North America.

British observers on American affairs thought much the same way. They claimed the Ohio country by right of the undefined western borders of some colonies. (Virginia, for example, claimed that its borders extended from the Atlantic to the Pacific.) By the late 1740s, land speculators, fur traders, and squatters from the mid-Atlantic colonies were already staking contesting claims to territory west of the Allegheny Mountains. A strong British prejudice against Roman Catholicism also shaped British perceptions of the French in North America. British writers described the French king and Roman Catholic pope as two sides of the same coin: despots bent on the political and spiritual subjugation of North America. But these same commentators also admired the centralized efficiency of New France's colonial government and compared it favorably to the division and competition that seemed to prevent the British colonies from cooperating in their Indian relations, fur trade, and westward expansion. In Document 3, a New York customs official enviously describes French success in winning Indian allies, while lamenting the British inability to do the same.

Colonial officials wrote about the contest for western land and the fur trade from a bird's-eye view, explaining how a remote borderland in America could affect the balance of power between European empires. The perspective was different from the ground. Documents 4 and 5 serve as reminders that the geopolitical interests of empires often resulted in acts of violence visited on people far removed from the centers of power. Document 4 illustrates the irreconcilable differences among colonial governments, squatters, and Indians on Pennsylvania's western frontier. Document 5 returns us to the Ohio country, where choices made in the fur trade could lead to unexpected and bloody reprisals.

Even in places far removed from the frontier, people interpreted such violence as evidence of an unavoidable showdown brewing between British Protestantism and French Catholicism, as Document 6 indicates.

Taken together, the sources in this chapter illustrate the combustible mix that human migrations, the fur trade, religious conflict, and imperial competition created in the Ohio country. From its start, the colonization of North America involved tensions among imperial powers, natives and newcomers, and the powerful and the poor. The conflicts these tensions produced were usually local and brief, but the confluence of imperial and regional interests revealed in this chapter made the Ohio country a particularly volatile place.

1

PIERRE-JOSEPH CÉLORON

Onontio in the Ohio Country

1749

The migration of eastern Indians into the Ohio country during the 1730s and 1740s made this region an attractive market for French and British fur traders. In places such as Logstown, located near modern Pittsburgh, mixed populations of Delaware, Shawnee, and Iroquois Indians planted new communities, forged new political ties, and committed themselves to defending their new homelands from outsiders. In 1749, the French governor-general of Canada, the Marquis de La Galissonière, sent a military expedition into the Ohio country to warn out British traders and renew alliances with the Indians there. In this passage from the journal of the expedition's commander, Pierre-Joseph Céloron de Blainville, Céloron records speeches he exchanged with the Indians at Logstown on behalf of the French governor-general, whom the Indians called Onontio (the Great Father).

From A. A. Lambing, ed., "Céloron's Journal," *Ohio Archaeological and Historical Quarterly* 29 (1920): 356–59.

Message of Monsieur the Marquis de la Galissonière to the nations of Chiningue [Logstown] brought by Monsieur de Céloron, the 10th of August. 1749, A belt.[1]

"The friendship which I entertain for you, my children, despite your estrangement from me, has induced me to send you Monsieur de Céloron to bring you a message and induce you to open your eyes with regard to the projects which the English form for your territories. Undoubtedly you are not aware of the establishments which they propose making thereon, which tend to nothing short of your total ruin. They hide from you their idea of establishing themselves therein in such a way as to render themselves masters of that territory, and drive you away, if I should let them do so.

"I ought then, like a good father who loves his children tenderly, and who, though far away from them, bears them all in his heart, to apprise them of the danger that threatens them, which is the design that the English have formed to take possession of your territories, no matter what wars I may have with the English. It is to your own advantage to observe the neutrality which you yourselves asked of me when you came to Montreal; to which demand I deigned to consent, and by this means you will preserve this peace which constitutes the happiness of the nations. As I know the English only inspire you with evil sentiments, and, besides, intend through their establishments on the Beautiful [Ohio] River, which belongs to me, to take it from me, I have summoned them to retire, and I have the greater right for doing so from the fact that it has been stipulated between the Kings of France and England, that the English should never repair thither for trade or aught else. It is even one of the conditions of the peace which we have just made together.[2] Moreover, the Chiefs of the Five Nations have told them not to pass over the mountains which form their boundaries. I do not wish to employ violence this time with regard to the English, I shall tell them quietly my determination that they should pay attention; for, if afterwards misfortunes befall them, they can only blame themselves.

"For you, my children, rest on your mats and do not enter into the disputes I may have with the English. I will take care for all that may be for your advantage, I invite you to come to see me next year. I will give

---

[1] When making diplomatic speeches or conveying diplomatic messages, Indians and colonial agents used belts and strings of wampum beads (manufactured from marine shells) to convey the importance and legitimacy of their words.

[2] The Treaty of Aix-la-Chapelle (1748), which ended the War of the Austrian Succession.

you marks of my friendship and will put you in such condition as not to regret those whom I advise you not to suffer among you. I will give you all the assistance of a kind father who loves you, and who will let you want for nothing. Those whom we shall bring to you will never covet your territories, either by purchase or usurpation; on the contrary, I will order them to maintain you thereon in spite of all the opposition, and your interests shall be common with mine, if you behave well. By this means you will be always tranquil and peace will reign in your villages. I would, my children, tell you the sentiments of your father before speaking to the English, whom I am going to look for to tell them to retire."

The council finished, they appeared well pleased with what I had told them, and went to their villages to prepare their answer, which I told them to do for the next day, having a long way to go, and the season being far advanced. This village is composed of Iroquois, Chanavaus [Shawnees] and of Loups [Delawares], for which cause the council lasted for more than four hours. Besides these three nations there are in this village Iroquois from the Sault St. Louis, from the Lake of the Two Mountains, and Indians from the Nepisiniques and the Abanakis, with Ontarios and other nations.[3] The gathering forms a bad village, which is seduced by the allurements of cheap merchandise furnished by the English, which keeps them in very bad disposition towards us. . . .

The 11th of August, the Indians came to give me their answers. If they are sincere, I believe Monsieur the Governor-General will be satisfied with them; but there is little reliance to be placed on the promise of such people, and the more so, as I have just said, since their personal interests make them look with favorable eyes on the English, who give them their merchandise at one-fourth the price. . . . It is true that the expenses of the English are not near so considerable as those which our merchants would be obliged to contract on account of the difficulty of the route. It is, however, certain that we can never regain the nations, except by furnishing them merchandise at the same price as the English; the difficulty is to find out the means?

These are the answers which the Indians of Chiningue made to the message of M. the Governor-General, the 11th of August, 1749.

"My father, we are very glad to see you to-day, and (are pleased) with the manner in which you regard us. The Commanders of Detroit and Niagara[4] had told us to go see Onontio; to-day you come yourself

---

[3] Indians from the *reserves* of Canada.
[4] French forts on the Great Lakes.

to invite us to go down. One must be insane not to pay attention to your word. By this string we assure you that all the nations who inhabit this river will go down next spring to hear the word from our father Onontio. Nothing will be able to turn us away from the sentiments which we now entertain. Even though but one person should remain, he will have the pleasure of seeing our father. The shoes which we wear at the thawing of the ice would not be able to carry us to Montreal; we pray him to make provision on that score so that we may find some at Niagara when we are passing that way.

"My father, have pity on us, we have no longer any ancient chiefs; it is only young people that now speak to you. Pardon the faults which we may commit because you, who are wisdom itself, also make some. You have expelled the English from this territory, and to this we heartily agree; but you ought to bring with you traders to furnish us with what we need. If you have pity for us, let us have the English so that they may render us the assistance which is necessary until the spring-time. You see in what an unfortunate plight we shall be, if you do not show us this kindness. Do not be surprised at not finding answers to your belts. Those you behold here are only young men who keep their pipes."[5] . . .

When the Council was finished I had the presents brought forward that I had destined for them. They were considerable enough. They were much flattered by them. I encouraged them anew to hold to what they had promised me, and above all to come to see Monsieur the Governor-General next year, assuring them that they would have reason to be well pleased with their reception at the hands of their father Onontio.

[5] In other words, the old chiefs who normally conducted diplomacy were not present at this time.

ROLAND-MICHEL BARRIN DE LA GALISSONIÈRE

A French Colonial Official Sizes Up the British

1751

*Roland-Michel Barrin de La Galissonière, the Marquis de La Galis-
sonière, was a French nobleman and naval officer who served as
governor-general of New France from 1747 to 1749. Although his tenure
as governor-general was brief, he initiated the aggressive measures taken
by France to assert its possession of the Ohio country after the War of the
Austrian Succession ended in 1748. After leaving office, he wrote a spirited defense of Canada's importance to France's world power, countering
critics who claimed that it was a costly and barren wasteland.*

We shall confine ourselves to regarding Canada as a barren frontier. . . .

This is precisely the case of Canada: it cannot be denied that this
Colony has been always a burthen to France, and it is probable that such
will be the case for a long while; but it constitutes, at the same time, the
strongest barrier that can be opposed to the ambition of the English.

We may dispense with giving any other proofs of this than the constant
efforts they have made, for more than a century, against that Colony.

We will add, however, that it alone is in a position to wage war against
them in all their possessions on the Continent of America; possessions
which are as dear to them as they are precious in fact, whose power is
daily increasing, and which, if means be not found to prevent it, will soon
absorb not only all the Colonies located in the neighboring islands of the
Tropic,[1] but even all those of the Continent of America.

Long experience has proved that the preservation of the major portion of the settlements in the Tropical islands is not owing so much to
their intrinsic strength, as to the difficulty of conveying troops thither

---

[1] The sugar colonies of the Caribbean.

From "Memoir on the French Colonies in North America," in E. B. O'Callaghan and Berthold Fernow, eds., *Documents Relative to the Colonial History of the State of New-York*
(Albany, N.Y.: Weed, Parsons, 1858), 10:223–24.

from Europe in sufficient numbers to subjugate or keep them, and of supporting such troops there; but if the rapid progress of the English Colonies on the Continent be not arrested, or what amounts to the same thing, if a counterpoise capable of confining them within their limits, and of forcing them to the defensive, be not formed, they will possess, in a short time, such great facilities to construct formidable armaments on the Continent of America, and will require so little time to convey a large force either to St. Domingo[2] or to the Island of Cuba, or to our Windward islands, that it will not be possible to hope to preserve these except at an enormous expense.

This will not be the case if we make a more energetic and generous effort to increase and strengthen Canada and Louisiana, than the English are making in favor of their Colonies; since the French Colonies, despite their destitute condition, have always waged war against the English of the Continent with some advantage, though the latter are, and always have been, more numerous; it is necessary to explain here the causes to which this has been owing.

The first is the great number of alliances that the French keep up with the Indian Nations. These people, who hardly act except from instinct, love us hitherto a little and fear us a great deal, more than they do the English; but their interest, which some among them begin to understand, is that the strength of the English and French remain nearly equal, so that through the jealousy of these two nations those tribes may live independent of, and draw presents from, both.

The second reason of our superiority over the English is, the number of French Canadians who are accustomed to live in the woods like the Indians, and become thereby not only qualified to lead them to fight the English, but to wage war even against these same Indians when necessity obliges.

Hence 'twill be seen that this superiority of the French in America is in some sort accidental, and if they neglect to maintain it, whilst the English are making every effort to destroy it, 'twill pass into the hands of the latter. There is no doubt but such an event would be followed by the entire destruction of our settlements in that part of the Globe.

This, however serious it may seem, would not be our only loss; it would drag after it that of the superiority which France must claim over England. . . .

---

[2] At this time, Saint-Domingue (modern Haiti) was the leading sugar producer in the Caribbean and France's most profitable New World colony.

We must not flatter ourselves with being able long to sustain an expenditure equal to theirs; no other resource remains then but to attack them in their possessions; that cannot be effected by forces sent from Europe except with little hope of success, and at vast expense, whilst by fortifying ourselves in America and husbanding means in the Colonies themselves, the advantages we possess can be preserved, and even increased at a very trifling expense, in comparison with the cost of expeditions fitted out in Europe. . . .

In fine [sum], Canada, the fertility whereof is wonderful, can serve as the granary of the Tropical Colonies, which, in consequence of the men they destroy, sell their rich products very dear. It is proved that the number of Canadians who die in these Colonies that are admitted to be the most unhealthy, is much less than that of European French.

All that precedes sufficiently demonstrates that it is of the utmost importance and of absolute necessity not to omit any means, nor spare any expense to secure Canada, inasmuch as that is the only way to wrest America from the ambition of the English, and as the progress of their empire in that quarter of the globe is what is most capable of contributing to their superiority in Europe.

3

ARCHIBALD KENNEDY

A British Colonial Official Sizes Up the French
1754

Archibald Kennedy migrated to North America from his native Scotland in the early eighteenth century, seeking opportunity in Britain's expanding empire. He settled in New York, where he worked as a customs official. During the early 1750s, he wrote several pamphlets decrying the state of colonial affairs, including the colonists' deteriorating Indian relations, weak defenses, and reluctance to submit to royal authority. He also warned his readers about a French plan to conquer America by

From [Archibald Kennedy], *Serious Considerations on the Present State of the Affairs of the Northern Colonies* (New York: James Parker, 1754), 3–7, 11–14.

taking possession of the territory west of the Appalachian Mountains.
Like many British observers, he described the methods used by the French
as underhanded and treacherous, but he also admired their success.
In the passages that follow, Kennedy suggests ways in which the British
might learn to imitate the French example.

As France has hitherto, by Means of Great-Britain chiefly, been pre-
vented from enslaving the World and Mankind, they are become of
Course our implacable and most inveterate Enemies, and of late every
where our Competitors in Trade, and, as one of the Links of their grand
System, Encroachers upon our Territories; regardless of all Faith,
Oaths, or Treaties, their national Polity being one continued Train of
Chicane[ry] and Deceit. . . .

That vast Sums have been expended upon their royal Geographers,
and Hydrographers, in order that their Maps and Sea Charts may quad-
rate with their political System of Encroachments upon the Territories
of other Nations, is apparent to the whole World; and thus by establishing their imaginary Rights by Pen and Ink, they are determined to confirm their Accuracy by a forcible Possession. Another Piece of Finesse
or French Policy, [is] that of burying Leaden Plates up and down this
Continent, with certain Inscriptions, in order to form new Pretensions;
but in this, I am told, they were discovered by some of our Indians, who,
tho' not pleased, were diverted with the Whim, as I am confident the
World must be with their other Project, being equally ridiculous.

What Figure we are like to make this Dispute; we, I say, who are so
nearly concerned in the Event, and who must become, in all Probability,
the first Sacrifice; we, to whom, in a great Measure, all this Imperti-
nence is owing, who by an ill-judged Frugality meanly neglected the
Preventing their first Intrusions at Crown-Point,[1] and that important
Pass at Niagara,[2] and some more of the like Kind, together with a total
Neglect of Indian Affairs, I shall not take upon me to determine. Nor
shall I enter into a Discussion of the Reasons of that Neglect, or to whom
owing, at this Time; this is not the Time to retrospect, we must now
look forward. Our Case at present is neither more nor less that this, viz.
That the French are now drawing a Line along the Borders of our Settlements in every Province, from the Mouth of the St. Lawrence, to the
Mouth of Mississippi, and building Forts to secure the most convenient

---

[1] The French built Fort Saint-Frédéric at Crown Point on Lake Champlain.
[2] Fort Niagara, the French post that guarded access to the portage around Niagara
Falls and travel between Lake Ontario and Lake Erie.

Passes on the Lakes, that form the Communication; by which they will effectually cut off all Intercourse and Traffic, between us and the Indians inhabiting the inland Countries; and likewise compel those who are Neighbours and Allies, by reason of the absolute Dependance they must have on the French for every thing they want, as well as for their Liberty of Hunting and Fishing, to fall under their Subjection, or starve. It therefore, I think, behoveth us at this Time to exert our utmost Endeavours, by all the Means in our Power, to prevent so bad a Neighbourhood. . . .

They have for many Years been indefatigable in their Endeavours to seduce our Indians; we on the other Side, have been as indolent as they could wish; and if ever they succeed in this Point effectually, they will have little else to do.

Regular Troops are of little Use here, further than to fight behind Walls; it is by Means of the Indians, and by them only, that any Stop can be put to those wicked Encroachments. And this is as yet very far from being either impossible or impracticable, if all Hands set heartily about it; the very French themselves openly upbraid us with our Indolence, and Divisions, which they acknowledge to be their greatest Security. It is evident therefore I think to a Demonstration, that if we continue to neglect our Indians much longer, or, if this Plan of a Congress for a Confederacy[3] should prove abortive through the Caprice of any Man, or Number of Men, or by any ill-judged Frugality, that we may from thence date the Commencement of the Dissolution and Destruction of these Colonies; As for my own part I sincerely believe the Indians will go off in a Body, and in that Case we shall most certainly be the first undone, Great-Britain will suffer, and all Europe will sooner or later feel the Effects of it. Those therefore, who are more immediately concerned, and with whom we have entrusted the Security of our Lives and Fortunes, have not a little to answer for to the present Generation, as well as to those who are to come after us, for their Conduct upon this critical Occasion.

Let us for once suppose the French, by their Fortifications and Lines of Communication, absolutely Masters, either by Force, or Friendship of the Indians; how easy a Matter would it be for them with a small naval Force to put us between two Fires? A small Force of regular Troops to attack Albany, and New-York, at the same Time, while their Blood-hounds are burning and massacring our Out-Settlements, is, in

---

[3] Kennedy is referring to the Albany Congress, an intercolonial treaty conference convened with the Iroquois confederacy in June 1754 to renew the Covenant Chain alliance and establish closer cooperation between the colonial governments in military and Indian affairs.

my humble Opinion, the Plan laid, and which they will put in Execution sooner or later, according as they become Masters of the Indians; and what a Catastrophe will this create! . . .

. . . The next Step that I would advise should be taken, is, that of erecting proper Fortifications in or near every one of the Indian Castles [Indian towns], with a Garrison of about 15 or 20 Men in each, with an approved Sergeant, two or three of which may be Smiths, in double Pay, with a few Field Pieces,[4] Spare Arms, Snow-Shoes (with which the French are always provided) small Hatchets and some Dogs of a proper Kind, to prevent Surprises in the Night.

This, I doubt not, the Indians would readily come into, as it would greatly incourage their Hunting, as well as their War Parties, and as it would be a Security for their old Men, Women, and Children, and a safe Retreat for themselves upon all Occasions; without such Security, they are impatient when Abroad, and seldom care to go far; besides the Loss of Numbers to the Service, upon any Emergency, who are detained at home for that Purpose. These Forts might at the same time answer all the Purposes of Truck or Trading-houses, to be divided by Lot amongst the contributing Colonies as far as they will go; and which, if properly stored with Indian Goods, and regulated to the Method in New-England,[5] would very soon create such an Intercourse and Connection between the remote Indian Nations and ours, as would turn out greatly to our Advantage. And one single independent Company would garrison the whole; and what a Trifle of a Charge would this be, in Comparison to the Advantages we might hope for and expect from it; and indeed it is my humble Opinion, that nothing less will effectually secure our Interest and Friendship with the Indians. . . .

This however is not all. If we intend to convince them [the Indians] that we are really in earnest, and that they should fight for us, we must fight along with them, and always to have some of our People to head their Parties; the French seldom fail of this Method: I should therefore advise the Establishing [of] an independent Company or two, in time of War, of an Hundred good Men each, with an Addition of five Indians from each [Iroquois] Nation, to be in constant Pay, Peace or War, as Rangers; one of the Companies from Connecticut would add Strength to the County of Albany; the Officers to be Men of some Distinction and Knowledge, and fully impowered to receive Complaints, and redress

---

[4] Small cannons and other artillery.
[5] At this time, Massachusetts maintained a system of frontier forts where Indian traders were publicly licensed and sold goods at fixed prices.

Grievances amongst the Indians; to be a Sort of a flying Camp, frequently moving from Nation to Nation, to head all Parties, and to command out as many Indians upon any Emergency as they may think proper; one Company of Rangers properly disposed, will be of more Use than three in Garrison. And here I shall beg Leave once for all to observe, that no Person employed in this Service be allowed to trade with the Indians, on the severest Penalties.

Thus our Indians being secured in an honest and fair Trade, their Castles secured, either for the Safety of their Families, or as a Retreat for themselves; and being well assured of our being in Earnest to support them upon all Occasions, as we have in former Days done, it is not [to] be doubted but that we shall very soon get into their good Graces and Friendship.

4

RICHARD PETERS

Tensions between Squatters and Indians

1750

During the 1740s and early 1750s, Scots-Irish colonists in Pennsylvania pushed past the Susquehanna River into the valleys of its western tributaries, clearing land and building homes. Mostly poor and newly arrived immigrants, these settlers had little money to pay for land and even less interest in honoring competing claims made to it by Indians or the heirs of William Penn. Their habit of squatting on land well beyond the authority of colonial officials irritated the Penn family proprietors and the Iroquois nations, who claimed that the Susquehanna region belonged to them. In this passage from July 1750, one of the Penn family's agents, Richard Peters, describes a joint effort by representatives of the Pennsylvania government and the Iroquois to remove these squatters before their actions led to open hostilities. To this day, the community located at this site is known as Burnt Cabins.

From *Pennsylvania Archives*, 8th ser. (1852–1856), 4:3321–25, 3330.

The Report of Richard Peters, Esq; Secretary of the Province of Pennsylvania, of the Proceedings against sundry Persons settled in the unpurchased Part of the Province aforesaid,

May it please your Honour,[1]

Mr. Weiser[2] and I having received your Honour's Orders to give information to the proper Magistrates against all such as had presumed to settle and remain on the Lands beyond the Kittochtinny Mountains,[3] not purchased of the Indians, in Contempt of the Laws repeatedly signified by Proclamations and particularly by your honour's late one; and to bring them to a legal Conviction, lest for Want of their Removal a Breach should ensue between the Six Nations of Indians and this Province:

We set out on Tuesday, the 15th of May last, for the new County of Cumberland,[4] where the Places, on which the Trespassers had settled, lay.

At Mr. Croghan's[5] we met with five Indians, three from the Shamokin,[6] two of which were Sons of the late Shickoalamy,[7] who transact the Business of the Six Nations with this government; two were just arrived from the Allegheny,[8] viz. one of the Mohock's Nation, called Aaron, and Andrew Montour,[9] the Interpreter at Ohio. Mr. Montour telling us he had a Message from the Ohio Indians and Twightwees[10] to this Government, and desiring a Conference, one was held on the 18th

---

[1] Peters is addressing his report to Pennsylvania lieutenant governor James Hamilton, who acted as the chief agent for the absentee governor and proprietor of the colony, Thomas Penn.

[2] Conrad Weiser was an Indian interpreter who often conducted business on behalf of the Penn family and the Pennsylvania government.

[3] The eastern foothills of the Allegheny Mountains west of the Susquehanna River.

[4] At this time, Cumberland County encompassed all of Pennsylvania west of the Susquehanna River.

[5] George Croghan was an Indian trader and interpreter who lived in western Pennsylvania.

[6] A populous Indian town at the juncture of the northern and western branches of the Susquehanna River (modern Sunbury, Pennsylvania).

[7] Shickellamy was an Oneida Indian who lived in Shamokin until his death in 1748, serving as the eyes and ears of the Iroquois confederacy there. He knew Weiser well, and the two of them worked cooperatively on diplomatic missions involving Pennsylvania and the Iroquois.

[8] The Allegheny River, which flows southwestward out of New York into western Pennsylvania.

[9] Like Croghan and Weiser, Andrew Montour was an Indian trader who occasionally worked as an interpreter for the Pennsylvania government.

[10] The Ohio Indians included Delawares, Shawnees, and Iroquois living along the Allegheny and Ohio rivers. The Twightwees were more commonly known as the Miamis and also lived in the Ohio country.

of May last, in the Presence of James Galbreth, George Croghan, William Wilson, and Hermanus Alrichs, Esquires, Justices of the County of Cumberland;[11] and when Mr. Montour's Business was done, we with the Advice of the other Justices, imparted to the Indians the Design we were assembled upon, at which they expressed great Satisfaction.

Another Conference was held, at the Instance [insistence] of the Indians, in the Afternoon, in the Presence of Mr. Galbreth and Mr. Croghan, before-mentioned, wherein they expressed themselves as follows:

"Brethren, We have thought a great deal of what you imparted to us, that you were come to turn the People off who are settled over the Hills; we are pleased to see you on this Occasion; and as the Council of Onondago[12] has this Affair at Heart, and it was particularly recommended to us by the Deputies of the Six Nations, when they parted from us last Summer, we desire to accompany you, but we are afraid, notwithstanding the Care of the Governor, that this may prove like many former Attempts; the People will be put off now, and next Year come again; and if so, the Six Nations will no longer bear it, but do themselves Justice: to prevent this therefore, when you shall have turned the People off, we recommend it to the Governor, to place two or three faithful Persons over the Mountains, who may be agreeable to him and us, with Commissions, impowering them immediately to remove every one who shall presume after this to settle there, until the Six Nations shall agree to make Sale of their Land." To Enforce this, they gave a String of Wampum, and received one in Return from the Magistrates, with the strongest Assurances that they would do their Duty.

On Tuesday, the 22nd of May, Matthew Dill, George Croghan, Benjamin Chambers, Thomas Wilson, John Finley and James Galbreth, Esquires, Justices of the said County of Cumberland, attended by the Under-Sheriff, came to Big Juniata, situate[d] at the Distance of Twenty-five Miles from the Mouth thereof,[13] and about ten miles North from the Blue Hills, a Place much esteemed by the Indians for some of their best hunting ground; and there they found five Cabbins or Loghouses, one possessed by William White, another by George Cahoon, another not quite finished in Possession of David Hiddleston, another possessed by George and William Galloway, and another by Andrew Lycon; of these

---

[11] These men were the local magistrates of Cumberland County and worked with Peters and Weiser to enforce the Penn family's proprietary land claims in this region.

[12] The Onondagas were one of the six nations in the Iroquois confederacy. The town of Onondaga (located near modern Syracuse, New York) served as the ceremonial and political center of the confederacy.

[13] The Juniata River is a western tributary of the Susquehanna River.

Persons, William White, George and William Galloway, David Hiddleston and George Cahoon appeared before the Magistrates, and being
asked by what Right or Authority they had possessed themselves of
those Lands, and erected Cabbins there on? They replied, by no Right
nor Authority, but that the Land belonged to the Proprietaries of Pennsylvania. They then asked, whether they did not know they were acting
against the law, and in Contempt of frequent Notices given them by the
Governor's Proclamations?

They said they had seen one such Proclamation, and had nothing to
say for themselves, but craved Mercy. Hereupon . . . the Under-Sheriff
was charged with them, and he took William White, David Hiddleston
and George Cahoon into Custody: but George and William Galloway
resisted, and having got at some Distance from the Under-Sheriff, they
called to us, "You may take our lands and Houses, and do what you
please with them; we deliver them to you with all our Hearts, but will not
be carried to Goal [jail]."

The next morning, being Wednesday, the 23rd of May, the said Justices went to the Loghouse or Cabbin of Andrew Lycon, and finding
none there but Children, and hearing that the Father and Mother were
expected soon, and William White and others offering to become Security jointly and severally, and to enter into Recognizance as well for
Andrew's Appearance at Court, and immediate Removal, as for their
own;[14] this Proposal was accepted, and William White, David Hiddleston and George Cahoon entered into a Recognizance of One Hundred
Pounds, and executed Bonds to the Proprietaries in the sum of Five
Hundred Pounds, reciting, that they were Trespassers, and had no Manner of Right, and had delivered Possession to me for the Proprietaries.

Then the Magistrates went to the Log-house or Cabbin of George
and William Galloway (which they had delivered up as aforesaid the
Day before, after they were convicted, and were flying from the Sheriff)
all the Goods belonging to the said George and William were taken out,
and the Cabbin being quite empty, I took Possession thereof for the
Proprietaries; and then a Conference was held, what should be done
with the empty Cabbin; and after great Deliberation, all agreed, that if
some Cabbins were not destroyed, they would tempt the Trespassers
to return again, or encourage others to come there, should these Trespassers go away; and so what was doing would signify nothing, since the
Possession of them at such a Distance from the Inhabitants could not be

[14] In other words, these men guaranteed Lycon's appearance in court, or they would
forfeit the bond they had paid.

kept for the Proprietaries; and Mr. Weiser also giving it as his firm Opinion of the Government, that if all the Cabbins were left standing, the Indians would conceive such a contemptible Opinion of Government, that they would come themselves in the Winter, murder the People, and set their Houses on Fire: On these Considerations the Cabbin, by my Order, was burnt by the Under-Sheriff and Company. . . .

The next day, being the 24th of May, Mr. Weiser and Mr. Galbreth, with the Under-Sheriff and myself, on our Way to the Mouth of Juniata, called at Andrew Lycon's, with Intent only to inform him, that his Neighbours were bound for his Appearance and immediate Removal, and to caution him not to bring himself or them into Trouble by a Refusal: But he presented a loaded Gun to the Magistrates and Sheriff, said, he would shoot the first Man that dared to come nigher [nearer]. On this he was disarmed, convicted, and committed to the Custody of the Sheriff. This whole Transaction happened in the Sight of a Tribe of Indians, who by Accident had in the Night-time fixed their Tent on that Plantation; and Lycon's Behaviour giving them great Offence, the Shickcalamies insisted on our burning the Cabbin, or they would burn it themselves; Whereupon, when every Thing was taken out of it (Andrew Lycon, all the while assisting) and Possession being delivered to me, the empty Cabbin was set on fire by the Under-Sheriff, and then Lycon was carried to Goal.[15] . . .

I leave it to Mr. Weiser (as he was joined with me by your Honour) to make his own Report; and shall only observe, that in all our Consultations, he (who is Indian interpreter for Virginia and Maryland as well as this Province, and must be supposed to know the Minds of the Indians the best) proceeded on this as a certain Truth, that if we did not in this Journey entirely remove these People, it would not be in the Power of the Government to prevent an Indian War.

[15] Lycon later returned to this land, where he was killed by a Delaware war party in 1756.

5

WILLIAM TRENT

The Fur Trade Turns Violent

1752

*The French regarded British fur traders in the Ohio country as trespass-
ers, but many Indians living in the region preferred to trade with the
British, who supplied greater quantities of goods at lower prices. This
competition erupted in violence in June 1752 at the Miami Indians' town
Pickawillany (near modern Dayton, Ohio), when a large force of French-
allied Indians and French soldiers took captive the British traders living
there, plundered their goods, and executed the town's pro-British chief.
This description of the raid was recorded by British fur trader William
Trent, who listened to an eyewitness report from one of the survivors.*

[July] 6th [1752]. We arrived at the lower Shawnees town,[1] where the
Indians received us very kindly, with the firing of guns, and whooping
and hollowing, according to their custom, and conducted us to the long
house [the council house], where, after they had given us victuals, they
inquired the news; we told them the next day we would let them know
everything.

Then Thomas Burney and Andrew McBryer,[2] the only two men that
escaped, when the town [Pickawillany] was attacked, came to us and
told us that 240 French and Indians, on the 21st of June, about nine
o'clock in the morning, surprised the Indians in the cornfields, and that
they came so suddenly on them that the white men, who were in their
houses, had the utmost difficulty to reach the fort.[3] Three not being
able to get to the fort shut themselves up in one of the houses. At this
time there were but twenty men and boys in the fort, including the white

---

[1] A Shawnee town at the juncture of the Scioto and Ohio rivers.
[2] Two traders who had witnessed the raid on Pickawillany.
[3] Traders often kept their own cabins in Indian towns they frequented. The fort was a
stockade that provided a common place of refuge in the event of attack.

From William Trent, *Journal of Captain William Trent from Logstown to Pickawillany,
A.D. 1752*, ed. Alfred T. Goodman (Cincinnati: Robert Clarke, 1871), 86–88.

men. The French and Indians having taken possession of the white men's houses, some of which were within ten yards of the fort, they kept a smart fire on the fort till the afternoon, and had taken three white men who had shut themselves up in one of the houses. . . . The French and Indians in the afternoon let the Twightwees[4] know that if they would deliver up the white men that were in the fort, they would break up the siege and go home.

After a consultation it was agreed by the Indians and whites that as there were so few men, and no water in the fort, it was better to deliver up the white men, with beaver and wampum, to the Indians not to hurt them, than for the fort to be taken, and all to be at their mercy. The white men were delivered up accordingly, except Burney and Andrew, whom the Indians hid. One of the white men that was wounded in the belly, as soon as they got him they stabbed and scalped, and took out his heart, and eat it. Upon receiving the white men they delivered up all the Indian women they had prisoners, and set off with the plunder they got out of the white men's houses, amounting to about three thousand pounds. They killed one Englishman and took six prisoners, one Mingoe[5] and one Shawanees killed, and three Twightwees; one of them, the old Pianguisha[6] king, called by the English Old Britain,[7] who, for his attachment to the English, they boiled, and eat him all up.

---

[4] The Twightwees were also known as the Miamis. They made up the bulk of the population at Pickawillany.

[5] The Mingoes were Seneca Indians who had resettled in the Ohio country.

[6] The Piankashaws were a branch of the Miamis.

[7] Known to the French as La Demoiselle, Old Briton was a Miami chief who favored British traders despite French warnings.

6

PHILIP READING

An Anglican Minister Warns of the French Catholic Peril in North America

1755

Ministers were prominent members of their communities in British North America, and their sermons served as an important means of spreading and interpreting news among the population. As representatives of the Church of England, Anglican ministers were especially inclined to conflate the Protestant faith with loyalty to the British crown and to interpret the Anglo-French tensions in the Ohio country as a spiritual struggle between Catholicism and Protestantism. These themes are evident in a sermon delivered by Philip Reading, an Anglican minister from Delaware, at Christ Church in Philadelphia on June 22, 1755, as General Braddock's army was marching toward Fort Duquesne.

Is not our Church, in this remote Corner of the Earth, too distant from her spiritual Rulers? Is not our Government in this newly cultivated Land, tho' not destitute of the royal Protection, yet removed from the royal Presence? . . . What shall we do for our Sister [the Church] in this her Day of Danger and Distress? What Course shall we pursue in Defence of our native Rights and Privileges, when these Dogs of Hell, Popish Superstitions and French Tyranny, dare erect their Heads, and triumph within our Borders? Shall we not rise up as one Man, and with united Hearts and Hands, vindicate our Religion and Liberties; our Protestant Religion, and our British Liberties? Shall we refuse any Aids of Wealth and Strength in our Power, when our distressed Country demands them at our Hands? . . .

. . . Indignation swells our Breasts, Love of Freedom inflames us, while we behold the Slaves of France, and the Inquisitors of Rome approaching to crush us. . . .

From Philip Reading, *The Protestant's Danger, and the Protestant's Duty* (Philadelphia: B. Franklin and D. Hall, 1755), 6, 10–11, 19–20, 27–28.

. . . The British Nation no sooner possessed this new World, than the Light of the Gospel shone forth with a pure, a reformed Lustre. Paganism fled at the Voice of the Ministers of Jesus. The Temples of the Heathen Idols soon became ruinous Heaps; and in their stead many goodly Churches were erected for the Worship of the one true God. Protestantism seemed to be a Blessing designed for this Part of America. That corrupt branch of Christianity, if it yet deserves the Name of Christian, called Popery [Roman Catholicism], made its Appearance only to be loaded with deserved Contempt. Yet contemptible as its Appearance was, confined tho' its Limits, such is the restless Temper of its Advocates, that no practicable Arts have, from Time to Time, been left unessayed for the Enlargement of its Borders. For this the Banners of France are now displayed, her Fleets have sailed, her Armies been transported, to establish at once the Thrones of Tyranny and Superstition in this Western World. Efforts black and horrid! Efforts destructive of every Thing sacred and good. . . .

And are not these the [French] Armies who are now invading our Borders? Are not these the Men who are this Day advancing in hostile Bands to our Habitations? What a Torrent of gloomy Ideas here rush impetuous on the prescient Mind! Do I see this goodly Land, so long the Seat of blooming Peace and Plenty, ravaged by the Sons of Rapine and Violence? Do I behold our fair Streets trod by the lordly Feet of French Conquerors, our well-built Mansions, deprived of their just Owners, become the Property of the servile Courtiers of an arbitrary Monarch? Do I see the Inquisitors Throne erected on the ruined Seat of banished Justice? Do I view our cultivated Fields sucking in the Blood of their antient Possessors, and pouring forth their rich Fruits to the greedy Vassal of some tyrannical Gallic Lord? Who is yonder Virgin shrieking in the Arms of a lustful Ravisher? Who is yonder Matron, weeping over the breathless Corpse of her slaughtered Husband, grieving for her Sons, hurried into Slavery and Banishment, and uttering fruitless Complaints to the Ears of insulting Enemies? Defend me Heaven! Frenzy burns up my very Soul at the Thought! Hide us ye Rocks! Cover us ye Mountains! Let not our Eyes behold this ghastly Scene of Desolation, Mourning and Woe! . . .

But, my Protestant Audience . . . the Cause I am now urging you to embark in, is the common Cause; the Principle I am now exciting you to act upon Christian and commendable. Not an inordinate Thirst of false Honour, to be acquired by Slaughter and Devastation; Not a Greediness to enlarge our Territories, or enrich ourselves with Spoils at the Expence of innocent and peaceable Neighbours; But an honest Desire to preserve in its due Channel what Encroachment and Usurpation would draw away; To assist in adjusting such a Ballance of Power, as may prevent ourselves becoming a Prey to an insatiable Devourer. . . .

Arise now, O God, and let thine Enemies be scattered. Do thou so bless our Sion,[1] the Vineyard which thine own Right Hand hath planted, and thy good Providence hitherto preserved, that neither the Gates of Hell, the Gates of Rome, nor the Gates of France, may ever prevail against her. Let there never be wanting a Race of Protestants to sway the British Scepter so long as the Sun and Moon endureth.

---

[1] Zion; that is, the sacred site of Jerusalem.

2

The Fog of War in the Ohio Country, 1753–1755

When describing decisions made on the battlefield, army officers and soldiers often talk about the "fog of war," a phrase that evokes the uncertainty and circumstance that can undo any military operation, no matter how well planned. The officers who devise military campaigns and the soldiers who carry them out never possess complete or entirely accurate information about the enemy. Instead, they must think on their feet, trying to anticipate the other side's objectives, resources, and maneuvers.

The Seven Years' War originated in such a fog in the region known as the Forks of the Ohio. Today, the city of Pittsburgh surrounds the point where the Monongahela and Allegheny rivers meet to form the Ohio River, but in 1753 the human populations closest to the Forks were several Indian towns dispersed along these waterways (see Map 1, page 2). The French and British knew that the Forks was a critical juncture for controlling the flow of people and goods between the Great Lakes and the Mississippi River. The French approached the Forks from the north, by way of Lake Erie. In 1753, French soldiers built two posts, Fort Presque Isle and Fort LeBoeuf, to guard the portage road between Lake Erie and French Creek, a tributary of the Allegheny River. At Venango, where French Creek flowed into the Allegheny, they built Fort Machault. By the spring of 1754, they were ready to move down the Allegheny to establish a fort at the Forks of the Ohio.

The British desperately wanted to beat them there. Pennsylvania traders were active in the Indian towns around the Forks region, but they lacked the organization, capital, and government support necessary to establish forts there. In Virginia, a group of land speculators known as the Ohio Company worked closely with the governor (who was one of its investors) to lay claim to the Forks before the French arrived there. In early 1754, workers hired by the Ohio Company began building a fortified storehouse at the Forks, promising the local Indians that it was only for the purpose of conducting the fur trade. They were soon overtaken by a much larger force of French soldiers, who sent the Ohio Company laborers packing and began constructing their own post on the site, Fort Duquesne. The Indians in the region—a mix of Shawnees, Delawares, and Iroquois—were suspicious of both the French and the British. They resented the French military presence in their homeland but had long-standing diplomatic and commercial ties with French traders and colonial officials. They valued the cheaper and more plentiful goods supplied by British traders but knew all too well that British settlers hungry for Indian land usually followed rapidly on the heels of the fur traders.

In the imperial contest for the Forks of the Ohio, each side tried to gather as much information as possible about the other and then respond accordingly. British and French governors and military officers were under orders from their superiors in London and Paris not to engage in aggressive actions that might start a war, but they were authorized to act defensively to protect their respective kings' claims to the disputed territory. Thus, each side played a diplomatic game of cat and mouse with the other, delivering letters and ultimatums backed up with shows of military force. Document 7 illustrates this game as George Washington, acting as the emissary of the governor of Virginia, confronted the French commander at Fort LeBoeuf. In Document 8, the French returned the favor by trying to deliver an ultimatum to Washington, but this time the war of nerves gave way to armed hostilities.

Documents 9 and 10 describe two successive, humiliating defeats suffered by British forces in the fog of war as they tried to force the French to withdraw from Fort Duquesne. In Document 9, Washington must face the consequences of bad weather, poorly disciplined troops, and his inability to read French. In Document 10, disaster ensues for a British army led by General Edward Braddock when it faces a French and Indian force in unfamiliar terrain. One disadvantage suffered by the British was their inability to convince the Indians of the Forks region to ally with them against the French. Washington learned that even the most pro-British Indians conducted diplomacy and warfare independently with the French. Braddock was impatient with what he considered to be the Indians' fickle and demanding nature and chose to work without them. Like many European military officers, Braddock described Indians as "savages" and presumed that they had nothing useful to teach professional soldiers about warfare. In Document 11, a Delaware chief named Shingas describes his encounter with Braddock and explains why his people decided to ally with the French instead.

In all the sources in this chapter, key figures involved in the outbreak of the Seven Years' War—British, French, and Indian—struggle to act on incomplete information. The British wanted to know what the French were up to and whether they had the resources to achieve their objectives. The French wanted to know the same about the British but were also concerned about the disposition of the Indians and anxious to dissuade them from their British inclinations. The Indians wanted to know which imperial power would provide them with the best trade but still leave them secure in the possession of their country. Whether making split-second decisions on the battlefield or conceiving strategies after deliberate consideration, none of these actors was able to comprehend fully the motives or objectives of the others.

7

GEORGE WASHINGTON

Encounter with the French

1753

When Robert Dinwiddie, the governor of Virginia, learned that the French were building forts along the route between Lake Erie and the Allegheny River, he sent a twenty-one-year-old militia officer named George Washington to warn them that they were trespassing on British territory and order them to leave. Washington undertook this mission in the late fall of 1753 with a small party of fellow colonists and Indians serving as his guides and interpreters. His most significant companion was Tanaghrisson, also known as the Half-King, an influential Seneca Indian from Logstown. Washington's journey was fraught with anxiety. Although treated well by the French officers he encountered at Fort Machault and Fort LeBoeuf, Washington feared attack from pro-French Indians, and early-winter snow and ice made travel extremely hazardous. After Washington's return to the colonial capital of Williamsburg in January 1754, Dinwiddie had Washington's journal printed to publicize the

From *Journal of Major George Washington, Sent by the Hon. Robert Dinwiddie . . . to the Commandant of the French Forces on Ohio* (Williamsburg, Va.: William Hunter, 1754), 16–19.

French presence in the Ohio country. In the passage that follows, Washington describes the intrigues that occurred between the French and his party during his stay at Fort LeBoeuf.

[December] 12th, [1753]. . . .

This Commander is a Knight of the military Order of St. Lewis, and named Legardeur de St. Piere. He is [an] elderly Gentleman, and has much the Air of a Soldier; he was sent over to take the Command, immediately upon the Death of the late General, and arrived here about seven Days before me.[1]

At 2 o'Clock the Gentleman that was sent for arrived, when I offer'd the Letter, &c. again; which they receiv'd, and adjourn'd into a private Apartment for the Captain to translate, who understood a little English; after he had done it, the Commander desired I would walk in, and bring my Interpreter to peruse and correct it, which I did.

13th, The chief Officers retired, to hold a Council of War, which gave me an Opportunity of taking the Dimensions of the Fort, and making what Observations I could. It is situated on the South, or West Fork of French Creek, near the Water, and is almost surrounded by the Creek, and a small Branch of it which forms a Kind of an Island; four Houses composed the Sides; the Bastions are made of Piles driven into the Ground, and about 12 Feet above, and sharp at Top, with Port-Holes cut for Cannon and Loop-Holes for the small Arms to fire through; there are eight 6 lb. Pieces [cannons] mounted, two in each Bastion, and one Piece of four Pound before the Gate; in the Bastions are a Guard-House, Chapel, Doctor's Lodging, and the Commander's private Store, round which are laid Plat-Forms for the Cannon and Men to stand on: There are several Barracks without [outside] the Fort, for the Soldiers Dwelling, covered, some with Bark, and some with Boards, and made chiefly of Loggs: There are also several other Houses, such as Stables, Smiths Shop, etc.

I could get no certain Account of the Number of Men here; but according to the best Judgment I could form, there are an Hundred exclusive of Officers, of which there are many. I also gave Orders to the People that were with me, to take an exact Account of the Canoes

---

[1] Captain Jacques Legardeur de Saint-Pierre was a seasoned military officer and diplomat in French Canada. He took over the command of Fort LeBoeuf after the death of Paul Marin de La Malgue, the previous commander of French forces in the Ohio country.

that were haled [hauled] up to convey their Forces down in the Spring, which they did, and told 50 of Birch Bark, and 170 of Pine, besides many others that were block'd out, in Readiness to make.

[Dec] 14th, As the Snow encreased very fast, and our Horses daily became weaker, I sent them off unloaded, under the Care of Barnaby Currin and two others, to make all convenient Dispatch to Venango, and there wait our Arrival if there was a Prospect of the Rivers freezing, if not, then to continue down to Shanapin's Town,[2] at the Forks of Ohio, and there to wait 'til we came to cross Aligany [Allegheny River], intending myself to go down by Water, as I had the offer of a Canoe or Two.

As I found many Plots concerted to retard the Indians Business, and prevent their returning with me, I endeavour'd all that lay in my Power to frustrate their Schemes, and hurry them on to execute their intended Design; they accordingly pressed for Admittance this Evening, which at Length was granted them, privately, with the Commander and one or two other Officers: The Half-King told me that he offer'd the Wampum to the Commander, who evaded taking it, and made many fair Promises of Love and Friendship; said he wanted to live in Peace, and trade amicable with them, as a Proof of which he would send some Goods immediately down to the Loggs-Town for them; but I rather think the Design of that is, to bring away all our straggling Traders they meet with, as I privately understood they intended to carry an Officer, etc. with them; and what rather confirms this Opinion, I was enquiring of the Commander, by what Authority he had made Prisoners of several of our English Subjects; he told me that the Country belonged to them, that no Englishman had a Right to trade upon those Waters; and that he had Orders to make every Person Prisoner that attempted it on the Ohio, or the Waters of it. . . .

[Dec] 15th, The Commandant ordered a plentiful Store of Liquor, Provision, etc. to be put on Board our Canoe, and appeared to be extremely complaisant, though he was exerting every Artifice that he could invent, to set our own Indians at Variance with us, to prevent their going 'til after our Departure: Presents, Rewards, and every Thing that could be suggested by him or his Officers. I can't say that ever in my Life I suffer'd so much Anxiety as I did in this Affair; I saw that every Stratagem that the most fruitful Brain could invent, was practiced, to win the Half-King to their Interest, and that leaving Him here was giving

---

[2] An Indian town near modern Pittsburgh that Washington had visited on his way to Fort LeBoeuf.

them the Opportunity they aimed at. I went to the Half-King, and press'd him in the strongest Terms to go: He told me the Commandant would not discharge him 'til the Morning. I then went to the Commandant, and desired him to do their Business, and complain'd of ill Treatment; for keeping them, as they were Part of my Company, was detaining me; which he promised not to do, but to forward my Journey as much as he could: He protested he did not keep them, but was ignorant of the Cause of their Stay; though I soon found it out: He had promised them a Present of Guns, etc. if they would wait 'til the Morning.

As I was very much press'd, by the Indians, to wait this Day for them, I consented, on a Promise, That nothing should hinder them in the Morning.

[Dec] 16th, The French were not slack in their Inventions to keep the Indians this Day also; but as they were obligated, according to Promise, to give the Present, they then endeavoured to try the Power of Liquor, which I doubt not would have prevailed at any other Time than this, but I urged and insisted with the King [the Half-King] so closely upon his Word that he refrained, and set off with us as he had engaged.

8

GEORGE WASHINGTON

Skirmish at Jumonville's Glen

May 1754

Washington returned to the Ohio country in the spring of 1754, this time leading approximately two hundred militiamen raised by Governor Dinwiddie to confront the French. Washington was intending to join the workmen already sent to build a fort at the Forks of the Ohio, but a larger French force beat him there, expelled the workers, and began building Fort Duquesne. Hearing advance reports of the French position, Washington decided to make his base camp at Great Meadows, about sixty miles southeast of the Forks. For the next several weeks, he and the French commander at Fort Duquesne, Captain Claude-Pierre Pécaudy, Seigneur de Contrecoeur, relied on Indian scouts and deserters to determine each

From Donald H. Kent, ed., "Contrecoeur's Copy of George Washington's Journal for 1754," *Pennsylvania History* 19 (1952): 20–22.

*other's strength and objectives. Their standoff turned into an armed con-
frontation when Washington led a detachment of his force in an attack on
a French detachment from Fort Duquesne led by Ensign Joseph Coulon
de Jumonville. The site of this engagement, a rocky wooded area near
Great Meadows, became known as Jumonville's Glen. In the following
passage, taken from a journal that the French would later seize, Washington reconstructs that fateful skirmish.*

May 27 [1754]. . . . About eight o'clock in the evening, I received an
express from the Half King,[1] who informed me that, as he was coming
to join us, they had seen along the road the tracks of two men which
went down into a gloomy hollow, and that he imagined that the whole
party[2] was hidden there. Instantly I sent out forty men; I ordered our
munitions put in a secure place, for fear that this was a stratagem of the
French to attack our camp. I left a guard there to defend it, and with the
rest of my men began to march through a heavy rain, with the night as
black as pitch and by a path scarcely wide enough for a man. We were
often astray for 15 or 20 minutes before we could find the path again,
and often we would jostle each other without being able to see. We continued our march all night long, and, May 28, about sunrise we arrived
at the camp of the Indians, where, after holding council with the Half
King, we decided to strike jointly.

Therefore, he sent out a couple of scouts to see where they were and
how they were arranged, and also to reconnoiter the vicinity, after which
we carried out our arrangements to surround them, and we began to
march in Indian fashion,[3] one after the other. We had advanced quite
near them according to plan, when they discovered us. Then I gave my
men orders to fire; my fire was supported by Mr. Wage's,[4] and my men
and his received the entire fire of the French during most of the action,
which lasted only a quarter of an hour until the enemy were routed.

We killed M. de Jumonville, commanding this party, with nine others; we wounded one and made 21 prisoners, among whom were
M. La Force, M. Drouillon, and two cadets. The Indians scalped the
dead, and took most of their arms. Afterward, we marched with the prisoners under guard to the camp of the Indians, where again I held council
with the Half King, etc. . . . Afterward, I proceeded with the prisoners.

[1] Tanaghrisson, who was leading Indians allied with Washington's troops.
[2] Jumonville was leading a party of thirty-five French soldiers.
[3] Single file, so as to hide the number in their party.
[4] Captain Thomas Waggoner, one of Washington's subordinate officers, who was
wounded in the skirmish.

They informed me that they had been sent with a summons for me to retire,[5] a specious pretense so that they could reconnoiter our camp and learn our forces and our situation. (See the summons and the orders.)[6] It was so evident that they had come to reconnoiter us that I admired their assurance in declaring to me that they had come as an embassy. Their instructions stated that they were to get information about the roads and rivers and about the country as far as Potomac.[7] Instead of coming as an ambassador should, publicly and in an open manner, they came with the greatest secrecy and looked for the most hidden retreats, much more suitable for deserters than for an ambassador. They camped there, they remained hidden there for two whole days, when they were no more than 5 miles from us. They sent out spies to reconnoiter our camp; the whole company re-traced its steps for two miles; two messengers were sent, as mentioned in the instructions, to warn M. de Contrecoeur of the place where we were and of our arrangement, so that he could send out his detachment to enforce the summons as soon as it should be given.

Besides, that was an escort worthy of a prince serving as ambassador, instead of which it was only a mere French petty officer; spies are not needed by an ambassador, whose dignity is always sacred. If they came with good intentions, why stay for two days five miles away from us without imparting the summons to me, or revealing anything relating to his embassy. That alone would be sufficient to give birth to the strongest suspicions, and we ought to do them this justice, that if they wanted to hide, they could not have chosen better than they did.

The summons is so insolent, and looks so much like bragging, that if two men had come to bring it openly, it would have been an excessive indulgence to have suffered them to return.

The Half King's opinion in this case is that they had evil designs, and that it was a mere pretext; that they had never pretended to come to us as anything but enemies, and that if we had been so foolish as to let them go, he would never help us to capture other Frenchmen.

They pretend that they called to us as soon as we were discovered. This is an absolute falsehood, for I was then at the head of the file going toward them, and I can affirm that, as soon as they saw us, they ran for their arms without calling, which I should have heard if they had done so.

---

[5] To leave the Ohio country.

[6] Washington is referring to papers seized from Jumonville, who was carrying a letter from Contrecoeur ordering Washington to withdraw his forces from French territory.

[7] Washington and his troops had started their trek into the Ohio country from a base on the Potomac River, at modern Cumberland, Maryland.

9

MARYLAND GAZETTE

Surrender at Fort Necessity

July 1754

Jumonville was wounded when Washington's men opened fire. Protesting that he was on a diplomatic mission, he tried to deliver a letter from Contrecoeur to Washington, but Tanaghrisson stepped forward and killed the French officer with a tomahawk blow to the head. The skirmish and death of Jumonville left Washington badly shaken. Knowing that the French had a numerically superior force at Fort Duquesne, he decided to fortify his position and wait for reinforcements. He dubbed the stockade and entrenchments built by his men at Great Meadows Fort Necessity. In the meantime, the French commander at Fort Duquesne sent a force of about six hundred soldiers and Indians, commanded by Jumonville's older brother, Captain Louis Coulon de Villiers, against Washington's position. In a letter published in a colonial newspaper, one of Washington's officers described the desperate situation that led to the fort's surrender.

July 1st [1754] . . . We set about clearing the Woods nearest to us, and carrying in the Logs, to raise a Breastwork, and enlarge the Fort. July 3rd, by Break of Day, we were alarmed by one of our Centries, who was shot in the Leg by the Enemy; and about nine, we received Intelligence, by some of our advanced Parties, that the Enemy were within four Miles of us, that they were a heavy numerous Body, and all naked. We continued to fortify, and prepare ourselves for their Reception. They came up with us before eleven o'Clock, and by their furious Attacks and superior Numbers, we expected that they would have attempted to storm us directly, and therefore answered them only with Musket Shot now and then. . . . At Night, they call'd to Parly, and we suspecting Deceit took but little Notice of it, until they repeated the same frequently, and then Mr. Van Braam[1] was sent to speak with them, who soon returned to assure us that they were in earnest. This was no disagreeable News

---

[1] Jacob Van Braam served as Washington's French interpreter.

From *Maryland Gazette*, August 29, 1754.

to us, who had received no Intelligence of the approach of our Convoys or Reinforcements, and who had only a Couple Bags of Flour and a little Bacon left for the Support of 300 Men. We had intended to have killed the Milch Cows which were our greatest Dependence before the Engagement, but had no Salt to preserve them, and they soon became the property of a superior Enemy. By the continued Rains, and Water in the Trenches, the most of our Arms were out of Order, and we had only a Couple of Screws in the whole Regiment to clean them.[2] But what was still worse, it was no sooner dark, than one-half of our Men got drunk.[3] Under these disadvantageous Circumstances, we agreed to the Articles of Capitulation,[4] which no Doubt you have seen. . . .

When Mr. Van Braam returned with the French Proposals, we were obliged to take the Sense of them by word of Mouth; It rained so heavily that he could not give us a written Translation of them; we could scarcely keep the Candle light to read them; they were wrote in a bad Hand, on wet and blotted Paper so that no Person could read them but Van Braam who had heard them from the mouth of the French Officer. Every Officer then present, is willing to declare, that there was no such word as Assassination mentioned; the Terms expressed to us were "the Death of Jumonville."[5] If it had been mentioned, we could have got it altered, as the French seemed very condescending, and willing to bring Things to a Conclusion, during the whole course of the Interview. Upon our insisting on it they altered what was more material to them, the Article relating to Ammunition, which they wanted to detain, and that of the Cannon, which they agreed to have destroyed, instead of reserved for their Use. Another Article, which appears to our Disadvantage, is that whereby we obliged ourselves not to attempt an Establishment beyond the Mountains: This was translated to us, "Not to attempt Buildings or Improvements, on the Lands of his Most Christian Majesty."[6] This we never intended; but denied that he had any Lands there, and therefore thought it needless to dispute that Point.

---

[2] The pouring rain on July 3 made it impossible for Washington's men to keep their guns in operable condition, and they lacked a sufficient number of gun screws to clean them.

[3] Expecting to be killed by the French and Indians in the morning, many of Washington's men broke into the fort's stores and consumed its rum supply.

[4] As discipline broke down within the fort and the situation turned hopeless, Washington negotiated articles of surrender with the French commander, relying on Van Braam as his interpreter.

[5] In the most controversial item of the articles of capitulation, Washington unwittingly accepted responsibility for the "assassination" of Jumonville, an act of war against France.

[6] The king of France.

. . . Thus by the evil Intention or Negligence of Van Braam, our Conduct is blamed by a busy World, fond of finding Fault without considering the Circumstances, or giving just Attention to Reasons which might be offered to obviate their Clamours. Let any of these brave Gentlemen, who fight so many successful Engagements over a Bottle, imagine himself at the Head of 300 Men, and laboring under all the Disadvantages above-mentioned, and would not accept of worse Terms than Col. Washington agreed to? . . . It appears to me, that if he did not, he might justly be said to be Accessary to the Destruction of so many Men, which would have been the inevitable Consequence of his mistaken Courage, or Obstinacy. You have no Reason to doubt but the whole Affair was well conducted, when the French, who had first orders to give no Quarter,[7] and to pay the Indians with our Scalps and Spoils, were the first who discovered an Inclination to Treat. That they had such Orders and intended no Quarter, is certain, from the Mouth of one of their own Officers.

[7] To take no prisoners; that is, to kill all enemies encountered.

10

BRITISH OFFICER

Disaster on the Monongahela
July 1755

Washington's surrender at Fort Necessity embarrassed the British crown and endangered its claim to the Ohio country. In the spring of 1755, two regiments of British regulars commanded by General Edward Braddock arrived in Virginia to march on Fort Duquesne and drive the French back to Canada. Braddock's force of approximately two thousand men departed from Fort Cumberland on the Potomac River (modern Cumberland, Maryland) in late May and made slow progress as it cut a road

From Charles Hamilton, ed., *Braddock's Defeat* (Norman: University of Oklahoma Press, 1959), 49–53.

through the hills of southwestern Pennsylvania. Frustrated by the delay, Braddock split his army in two and moved forward with the half unencumbered by the supply train. On the morning of July 9, this contingent crossed the Monongahela River and moved within ten miles of Fort Duquesne. The French commander, Contrecoeur, sent a combined force of Indians and soldiers to stop the British. This description of the battle is from an anonymous account written by one of Braddock's officers.

Wednesday July the 9th [1755]. As we were to cross the Mona[n]gahela that day & so near the Fort as we were drawing, it was found absolutely necessary to detach a party to secure the crossing. Accordingly Lieutenant Colonel Gage[1] with 300 Men & the Grenadier Companys[2] with two pieces of Cannon marched before day break and before the road was cleared. At day break the whole detachment marched, tho slowly, having a great deal of trouble with the road; after 5 Miles march we came to the first crossing of the river[3] which was extreamly fine having a view of at least 4 Miles up the river & the breadth about 600 Yards; near this first crossing our advanced party scared some Indians from their holes, finding many spears & their fires newly burning. From this crossing to the other was near two miles & much the finest of the two; on the other side of the second crossing the advanced party had halted at Fraziers house[4] close to the bank which was very steep & took us two hours to make it passable for the carriages. The General now thinking the dangerous passes were over did not suffer the advanced party to proceed any farther than the distance of a few Yards from the main body. It was proposed to strengthen the flanks but this was unhappily rejected.

Between 12 & 1 after we had marched 800 Yards from the river our first flank upon the left was fired on & every Man of them killed or wounded; the alarm quickly became general & the fire was brisk from right to left, the Indians were all planted behind trees & fired with the utmost security; the ground where the Enemy was posted was rising and advantagious. Upon our right were a couple of immense large trees fallen on each other which the Indians were in possession of & anoyed

---

[1] Thomas Gage, who would later serve as commander in chief of the British army in North America and the last royal governor of Massachusetts.

[2] Grenadiers were an elite body of infantry within the British army.

[3] Braddock crossed the river in two places that day to avoid exposing his force in some hazardous narrows.

[4] A former British fur-trading post run by John Fraser, one of the British traders who had gone into the Ohio country in the 1740s.

us from very much; but an Officer & a party of men soon dislodged them, & by a pretty brisk fire kept our right tollerably easy; the Guns which were all rather to the left fired both round & grape shott[5] doing great execution. The Indians, whether ordered or not I cannot say, kept an incessant fire on the Guns and killed the Men very fast. These Indians from their irregular method of fighting by runing from one place to another obliged us to wheel from right to left, to desert the Guns and then hastily to return & cover them.

At the first of the firing the General [Braddock] who was at the head of the detachment came to the front, & the American Troops though without any orders run up immediately some behind trees & others into the ranks & put the whole in confusion. The men from what storys they had heard of the Indians in regard to their scalping and Mawhawking,[6] were so pannick struck that their Officers had little or no comand over them, & if any got a shott at one the fire immediately ran through the whole line though they saw nothing but trees; the whole Body was frequently divided into several parties, & then they were sure to fire on one another. The greatest part of the Men who were behind trees were either killed or wounded by our own people, even one or two Officers were killed by their own Plattoon. Such was the confusion, that the men were sometimes 20 or 30 deep, & he thought himself securest who was in the Center; during all this time the Enemy kept a continual fire and every shot took place. The General had given orders that they should fire in Platoons (which was impossible to be effected) which would not have answered at all as the Enemy were situated. Within about two hours & an half the Men were obliged (or at least did) retreat three or four times & were as often rallied. We found that we should never gain the day unless we dislodged them from the rising ground, upon which Lieutenant Colonel Burton[7] with the Grenadiers pushed & attempted the Hill; for sometime we were in hopes of their success, but some Shot killing 2 or 3 of them, the rest retreated very fast, leaving their Officers (entreating & comanding but) without any regard to what they said. The Indians were scalping at the begining of the affair which we heard was a sign they were dubious of Success but [it] is certain they never gave ground. General Braddock who was in the heat of the Action the whole time, was greatly exposed; he had 4 horses shot under him &

---

[5] Grapeshot consisted of canisters of small iron balls fired from cannons. It was designed to explode over a wide area and inflict casualties on massed forces.

[6] A reference to the Mohawks, regarded by the British as the fiercest of Indian warriors.

[7] Lieutenant Colonel Ralph Burton was one of Braddock's subordinate officers.

shot through several parts of his cloaths; at the latter end of the affair an unlucky Shot hit him in the Body which occasioned his death in 3 or 4 days afterwards. Sir Peter Hackett[8] was killed at the beginning & many more Officers.

After the Men retreated from the hill, they made some stand & the Cannon kept a tollerable good fire, but very soon for want of sufficient Guard to it, the Men were obliged to leave them. During this time the Wagoners who imagined things would turn out badly, had taken the gears from their Horses & galloped quite away so that if Fortune had turned in our favour we had not one horse left to draw the Train forwards. However, after about 4 hours of incessant firing & two thirds of the Men killed or wounded, they as if by beat of Drumm turned to the right about & made a most precipitate retreat every one trying who should be the first. The Enemy pursued us butchering as they came as farr as the other side of the River; during our crossing they Shot many in the Water both Men and Women, & dyed the stream with their blood, scalping & cutting them in a most barbarous manner. On the other side of the river we most of us halted to resolve on what to do; but the Men being so terrified desired to go on, nay indeed they would; melancholy situation! Expecting every moment to have our retreat cut off (which half a dozen men would easily have done) & certainty of meeting no Provisions for 60 Miles. I must observe that our retreat was so hasty that we were obliged to leave the whole Train; Amunition, Provision & bagage to the plundering of the Indians. The Mens wounds being fresh, many of them retreated with us though in the utmost agonies. In making the road we [had] marked the trees on each side of it, which we found of very great Use to us in our retreat, for being obliged to keep marching the whole night through a continued Wood, the people frequently lost their way, & had nothing to put them right except feeling for the Marks; nevertheless many of the Rear lost their Way, & of the wounded entirely lost.

---

[8] Sir Peter Halkett was one of Braddock's subordinate officers.

11

SHINGAS

A Delaware Chief Explains
Why the Indians Went to War
1755

Braddock's defeat on the Monongahela and the rapid retreat of the surviving half of his army left the mid-Atlantic frontier exposed to enemy attack, especially in Pennsylvania, which had no militia and no fortifications. Indian and French war parties began raiding settlements and homesteads in the Susquehanna Valley in the fall of 1755, killing civilians, slaughtering livestock, burning homes and barns, and taking many captives. One such raid devastated the community at Great Cove (modern McConnellsburg, Pennsylvania), where Charles Stuart was taken captive. He spent two years living among the Delawares, claiming to have been spared death because of the hospitality he had previously shown to Indians, until he finally gained his freedom in a prisoner exchange between the French and British. In the account of his captivity written for British military commanders excerpted here, Stuart recalls a speech delivered by the Delaware chief Shingas, who had led the raid on Great Cove and blamed the Ohio Indians' disaffection on the conduct of the British.

Riseing up From his seat with Appearance of Deep Concern on his Countenance he [Shingas] addressed his Prisoners with Great Solemnity, Telling them that he was sorry For what had happened Between them and the English But that the English and not the Indians were the Cause of the Present War—he then Proceeded to give account of those Causes and said—That he with 5 other Chiefs of Delaware Shawnee & Mingo Nations (Being 2 from Each Nation) had applied to Gen Braddock[1] and Enquired what he intended to do with the Land if he Could

---

[1] Shingas is describing a treaty council held at Fort Cumberland before Braddock commenced his march toward Fort Duquesne.

From Beverly W. Bond Jr., ed., "The Captivity of Charles Stuart, 1755–57," *Mississippi Valley Historical Review* 13, no. 1 (June 1926): 63–65.

drive the French and their Indians away. To which Gen Braddock replied that the English Shoud Inhabit & Inherit the Land, on which Shingas asked Gen Braddock whether the Indians that were Friends to the English might not be Permitted to Live and Trade Among the English and have Hunting Ground sufficient to Support themselves and Familys as they had no where to Flee To But into the Hands of the French and their Indians who were their Enemies (that is Shingas' Enemies). On which Gen Braddock said that no Savage Should Inherit the Land. On receiving which answer Shingas and the other Chiefs went that night to their own People—To whom they Communicated Gen Braddock's Answer And the Next Morning Returned to Gen Braddock again in hopes he might have Changed his Sentiments and then repeated their Former Questions to Gen Braddock again and Gen Braddock made the same reply as Formerly. On which Shingas and the other Chiefs answered That if they might not have Liberty To Live on the Land they would not Fight for it. To which Gen Braddock answered that he did not need their Help and had No doubt of driveing the French and their Indians away.

On which Shingas with the other Chiefs went away from Gen Braddock To their People To whom they Communicated what had passed Between them & Braddock, at which they were very much Enraged and a Party of them went Immediately upon it and Join'd the French. But the Greater Part remained neuter [neutral] till they saw How Things wou'd go Between Braddock and the French in their Engagement. And they made it their Business to draw nigh [near] the Place where the Engagement Happened that they might see what Passed at it and were still in hopes that the English wou'd be Victorious. But after the French had ruined Braddocks Army they immediately compelled the Indians To join them and let them know that if they refused they wou'd Immediately cut them off. On which the Indians joined the French for their own Safety—They However sent Capt Jacobs[2] with some other Indians to Philadelphia to hold a treaty with the Government. But on their returning home from Philadelphia without meeting with the necessary Encouragement the Indians agreed to Come out with the French and their Indians in Parties to Destroy the English Settlements.[3] The French having appointed 1400 French and Indians to come out in Small Parties for that Purpose. . . . Thus begun the War between the English and the Indians and Such have Been the Consequences thus far.

[2] Another Delaware chief from the Forks region.
[3] An embassy of Ohio Indians met with the Pennsylvania governor in Philadelphia about one month after Braddock's defeat but were unable to secure military support from the colonial government.

After which Shingas Proceeded to Say that they did not want to Carry on the War against the English and were now willing again To make Peace with them and restore all their Captives and Everything Else they had from them Provided the English wou'd Comply with the Following Proposals Vizt 1st the English shou'd send 5 men among the Indians who shou'd live well at the Indians expence with them, But [should] work for them without any other Pay from the Indians than Supporting Said Workmen and their Familys with Provisions and all other necessaries that they stood in need of. The Business said men were to Be Employed in were Makeing of Powder [gunpowder], Smelting of Lead from the Ore, and Indians would Engage not only to find them Lead Mines But mines of Every other Metal that was necessary—Weaving of Blanketts—Makeing and Mending Guns for them—and . . . the Other Man was to Be Employed in Makeing of Iron—The 2nd Condition was that the English should Come and Settle among them with their Families and Promote Spinning for Shirts and in General should Bring all Kinds of Trades among them that they might be Supplied with what they want near home, and that they and the English shou'd Live Together in Love and Friendship and Become one people. But the Indians did not Insist nor Desire that the English shou'd be obliged to Intermarry with them. That on these Terms they wou'd be glad to Be at Peace with the English, and desired the Prisoners to write the Governor of Pennsylvania about it.

3

American Ways of War

Combatants in the Seven Years' War in North America engaged in two types of warfare. In the first, armies numbering in the thousands fought for possession of key portages and passageways along the interior waterways that connected British North America and French Canada. The war started over one such location, the Forks of the Ohio, but then moved northward to the New York–Canadian frontier, where waterways associated with Lake Champlain and Lake Ontario provided routes of invasion for the opposing armies. Military campaigns in this region required moving troops, along with their artillery and supply trains, from the eastern seaboard through densely forested wilderness. The Seven Years' War brought an unprecedented scale of military engineering to colonial America, as soldiers and civilians labored to build roads, watercraft, and defensive fortifications. Britain and France sent thousands of soldiers across the Atlantic to fight these battles, but both sides also recruited heavily among their colonial populations, giving thousands of colonists their first exposure to European-style warfare.

Eighteenth-century armies practiced the art of siegecraft. Most famously summarized in the writings of French military engineer Sébastien Le Prestre de Vauban, siegecraft centered on the construction and defense of forts intended to protect cities, ports, or strategic routes of travel. Such forts, built according to Vauban's specifications, were designed to garrison troops and civilian laborers and to house artillery for fighting off an attack. When under siege, the commanding officer's goal was to withstand the attacking army's advance long enough for reinforcements to arrive and lift the siege. An officer charged with taking such a fort also followed Vauban's directions. His army worked around the clock to dig trenches and build artillery batteries that would allow soldiers to approach the fort under covering fire until they were able to breach its walls. In addition to fighting each other, the opposing armies fought time. As a siege dragged on, the armies were weakened by diminishing provisions and ammunition, physical and mental exhaustion, and, most significantly, diseases spread by poor sanitation, such as dysentery.

Siegecraft involved marshaling troops, laborers, and materiel on a grand scale. Armies that conducted such operations had to be professionally trained with high degrees of specialization and hierarchy. In Europe, their officers subscribed to an aristocratic code of conduct that reflected their notions of professionalism and gentility. Foot soldiers were recruited from the geographic and economic margins of society, lured into service by cash bounties and regular pay, and kept there by coercive discipline and their own esprit de corps.

The professionalization of European warfare was also reflected in a shared system of negotiation between opposing armies. Under flags of truce, the opposing commanders parleyed, or conferred, with each other. A fort's defending army was expected to put up a fight, but it need not resist to the last man. Once a fort's walls were breached, a commander who had lost hope of reinforcements could negotiate a capitulation that included the "honors of war," concessions from the victorious army that allowed the defeated enemy to keep its arms and guaranteed it protection from plunder and assault. A defending army that refused such generous terms could expect to receive no quarter if the attacking army had to endure the heavy casualties associated with a final assault on the fort.

The second kind of warfare practiced in North America was *la petite guerre*. Known more commonly today as guerrilla or irregular warfare, it involved fighting on a much smaller scale and with tactics that relied on speed and surprise. British colonists referred to it as "the skulking way of war" and associated it with Native Americans, whom they believed to be naturally treacherous and cowardly, and therefore inclined to ambush civilians rather than face armed adversaries in open battle. French colonists were less judgmental of Indian methods. In Canada, militiamen and *troupes de la marine* adopted the methods of their native allies and joined them in conducting surprise raids on isolated settlements, calculated to maximize the number of captives taken while minimizing their own casualties.

These combined Indian and French war parties covered great distances because they did not need to bring along supply trains or artillery. Neither did they rely on an elaborate hierarchy of command or corporal punishment to operate effectively in the field. Indian warriors went to war for reasons culturally significant to them: to gain reputation and influence among their peers, to avenge the deaths of their kin, to take plunder and trophies (such as scalps) that proved their prowess in battle, and to bring captives home. In their conflicts with Indians, colonial militiamen learned to adopt some of these tactics. They took scalps from the enemy dead and conducted scorched-earth campaigns against Indian towns. Like Indians, colonial soldiers who served alongside European armies in North America exhibited little patience for the backbreaking labor, fatigue, and long-term exposure to danger involved in siegecraft. Desertion by native and colonial allies was a constant problem for the European officers who conducted such campaigns.

The sources in this chapter illustrate the clashing cultural values and military practices involved in siegecraft and *la petite guerre*. In Document 12, the French commander of Fort Niagara details the unfolding of a Vauban-style siege there, but one complicated by the presence of a large number of Indians on each side of the fight. In Documents 13 and 14, the methods of *la petite guerre* are illustrated and described by colonial militiamen and Indian warriors fighting on the Pennsylvania frontier. Documents 15 and 16 bring two more perspectives to the fighting: that of a British woman working as part of Braddock's ill-fated army and that of a New England soldier serving in another disastrous British campaign, the assault on Fort Carillon at Ticonderoga in 1758. In Document 17, an American officer blends European and Native American tactics in the rules of war he gave to his company of rangers fighting along the Lake Champlain frontier. Considered together, these sources reflect the ways in which Native American, colonial, and European methods of warfare clashed and combined with one another during the Seven Years' War.

12

PIERRE POUCHOT

Siegecraft at Fort Niagara
1759

Fort Niagara was one of the most important French posts in North America, linking New France's population center in the St. Lawrence River valley to its commercial and military hinterlands in the western Great Lakes and Ohio country. In July 1759, a British army that included nine hundred Iroquois warriors laid siege to Niagara, slowly advancing its trenches and artillery toward the fort's walls while the garrison awaited reinforcements from French posts on Lake Erie. The three-week siege unfolded in typical eighteenth-century fashion, with artillery barrages and parleys for negotiation, but with the added twist that neither the French nor the British were entirely certain which side, if either, the Indians inside and outside the fort would ultimately take. Captain Pierre Pouchot commanded Fort Niagara at the time of the siege. His journal details parleys with the British and Iroquois as well as the physical and psychological pressures suffered by the soldiers and civilians inside the fort.

About ten o'clock a white flag appeared in the clearing, and M. Pouchot sent out to meet it with caution. They brought in a captain of the Royal Americans,[1] with his eye bandaged,[2] and led him through the thickest and most encumbered brush wood. He produced in the room of the commandant,[3] after the bandage was removed, a letter from the

---

[1] The Royal Americans were a regiment formed in the 1750s to recruit colonial Americans into the British army.

[2] Blindfolded, to prevent him from gaining intelligence about the fort and its garrison.

[3] As was often typical for eighteenth-century European military officers writing reports for their superiors, Pouchot refers to himself in the third person throughout this account but uses the first person plural ("us," "we," and "our") when referring to the French force collectively.

From Pierre Pouchot, *Memoir upon the Late War in North America between the French and English, 1755–1760*, trans. and ed. Franklin B. Hough (Roxbury, Mass.: W. E. Woodward, 1866), 1:166–67, 169–74, 176, 180–81, 185–86, 190, 194–96.

Brigadier general Prideaux,[4] in which he said, the king of England having given him the government of Fort Niagara, had sent him thither, if
necessary to compel its surrender by the superior forces he had with
him. M. Pouchot replied, that he did not understand the English, and that
he had no reply to make.

He had, however, well understood the letter. The officer insisted
upon the strength of his forces. M. Pouchot replied that the king had
entrusted him with the place, which he found himself in condition to
defend; that he hoped M. Prideaux could never enter it, and that at least
before he made any terms with him, he wished an opportunity of gaining their esteem. He invited the officer to breakfast, and then sent him
back with his eyes bandaged and the way he came. . . .

On the 10th it rained, with a fog at daybreak, which prevented us
from observing the field most of the day. We then perceived a parallel[5]
of more than 300 toises[6] which beginning at about the middle of the
front of the fortifications, extended to the left on the side towards the
lake. . . .

We battered both ends of this parallel with four pieces of cannon,
although it rained quite hard. The enemy appeared to labor with ardor.
In the night, we fired cannon on the left, as we thought they would try to
prolong their work upon that side. At noon, M. Chabert and Joncaire,[7]
his brother, arrived with seventy persons, several of them women,
and some Indians. Three were Iroquois, among whom was the chief
Kaendaé.[8] The Indians were very quiet.

On the morning of the 11th, we observed that this parallel was a little
extended to the left, and we fired upon it vigorously. They did not venture to push it further, but during the day labored to perfect it, and we
observed that they were at work on the batteries. We incommoded them
as much as possible with our artillery. . . .

. . . Kaendaé the Iroquois chief, asked leave to go out to speak to the
Indians of his nation. M. Pouchot thought he ought not to deny him, but
rather hoped, through the aid of this Indian, to at least induce some of
the Senecas to abandon their army.[9] The Iroquois accepted this parley,

---

[4] General John Prideaux commanded the British forces at Niagara.

[5] A trench dug parallel to the defensive ditch around the fort.

[6] An archaic French unit of measurement; one toise equaled approximately six feet.

[7] The brothers Philippe-Thomas de Chabert and Daniel-Marie Joncaire were French
fur traders, Indian agents, and military officers with long-standing ties to Fort Niagara
and the Seneca Indians.

[8] Kaendaé was a Seneca chief and leader of the pro-French Senecas at Niagara.

[9] To desert the British.

at the end of the clearing, and the result was, that the Five Nations sent two deputies to M. Pouchot, to learn his views concerning themselves. They demanded a safe conduct upon the word of M. Joncaire, whom they regarded as one of their chiefs. They were led with their eyes blinded into the room of the commandant. . . . These deputies said they did not know how they had got involved in this war, and that they were ashamed of it. M. Pouchot asked them what occasion for war he whom they had named Sategariouaen[10] (The midst of good affairs), had given them, and said that he had never deceived them. He expressed his surprise at seeing the Iroquois in the English army, and among them many who had shown him great affection; that they could judge from his manner of fighting that he would not spare his enemies, and his heart bled at the thought that he might strike some others besides the whites against whom he fought. He invited them to mingle no more in their quarrels, and he assured them that nothing was nearer his heart than this. He ended by saying, that all the upper nations[11] were coming constantly to his aid, and should they find themselves bent upon shedding their blood, he promised to interpose his authority to induce them to make peace. He gave them a great belt to carry these words to their nation. . . .

. . . These harangues lasted until nine o'clock in the evening, when we sent the deputies out with their eyes bandaged. They promised to return on the morrow and bring their reply. . . .

On the 12th . . . in the morning, Kaendaé again asked leave to go out and hold a council with the chiefs of his nation. M. Pouchot did not offer to oppose him, but gave notice, that he should not suspend any of his operations, because the whites would take advantage of this interval to labor.[12] . . .

At three o'clock in the afternoon, Kaendaé returned with an Onondaga chief named Hanging Belt, and two Cayugas. They presented a large white belt[13] to M. Pouchot, to reply to the one he had sent. They said: "We have heard your words, and they are true. Our part is taken, we will quit the English army, and to prove this, we will go and encamp at La Belle-Famille."[14] They thanked him for having given them so good advice, and hoped there would be left no rancor between them. They

---

[10] Like many military officers, Pouchot had received an Indian name in previous diplomatic councils by which the Indians addressed him.

[11] Algonquian Indian nations from the *pays d'en haut.*

[12] Pouchot was concerned that while the Indians engaged in their negotiations, the British would extend their trenches.

[13] A white wampum belt represented peace.

[14] A spot upriver, not far from the fort.

promised to be henceforth quiet. The council of Kaendaé with the Iroquois was held in the presence of Johnson,[15] to whom this chief spoke fiercely, reproaching him for having embarked his nation on a bad cause. Johnson smiled and regarded this reproof as a joke.

By another belt, they asked that Kaendaé, the women and the children of the Iroquois who were in the fort, should come out with Joncaire, whom they regarded as one of themselves, so that the kettles[16] should not fall on their heads. They were especially anxious about Kaendaé, who was charged with their business with the Indians of other tribes, and spoke all their languages. . . .

To explain all these parleys it should be observed that the English by night employed the Indians to cover their laborers. Our fire from the covered way[17] disturbed them much. They had lost eight or nine of their people. M. Pouchot who knew the character of these nations was not sorry to find the occasion for relieving himself of nine hundred men,[18] whose insults he feared more that the English, on account of their number, and the knowledge they had of the place. In retaining some of their chiefs in the fort, with the women, and several warriors of foreign tribes, if they were harmed these same Indians would have to answer to their nations, or those whom they might have offended. They were therefore pleased with the idea which this occasion offered, of remaining neutral awaiting events. The English, on their part, did not dare to forbid these interviews of the Indians. They only sought to turn them to the best account. . . .

On the 18th, in the morning, we did not notice that the enemy had pushed his works forward, and he appeared to be busy repairing the damages that our artillery had occasioned. In the evening a great smoke arose from their trenches, one of our shot having set fire to one of their powder magazines. On this day, general Prideaux was killed in the trench.[19] The fire was very brisk on both sides, and increased towards evening, as well the cannon as the mortars and howitzers, by which we were greatly distressed, having, many soldiers wounded and some killed. . . .

The enemy on the night of the 22d and 23d, pressed their trenches forward . . . and through the night fired heavily with their artillery, both

[15] Sir William Johnson, a colonial Indian agent and Prideaux's second-in-command.

[16] Artillery fire from the British.

[17] A defensive position outside the fort, from which the French fired on the British trenches.

[18] In other words, Pouchot was pleased that the nine hundred Iroquois warriors with the British troops had agreed to withdraw to La Belle Famille.

[19] Prideaux was killed when he stepped in front of a mortar shell fired from his own lines. Johnson took over as commander of the British forces.

grape [grapeshot] and balls upon the breach, as also with musketry, and threw many bombs. We replied to them from our fort, but our arms were in so bad a condition, that among ten guns scarcely one could be used, and on the next day there remained not more than a hundred fit for use, notwithstanding all the repairs daily made. Seven smiths or armorers were constantly employed in mending them. The domestics and wounded were employed in washing them. The women, as we have said, attended the wounded and sick, or worked sewing cartridges or sacks for earth. . . . The Canadians[20] no longer wished to hold this place on account of the sharpness of the enemy's fire. . . .

We could no longer induce the Canadians to fire into the embrasures[21] at the enemy, by which they would have been greatly deranged. The fire was too much for them. Those who were placed at any point crouched down to cover themselves, and were soon asleep, in spite of all that the officers and sergeants could do to induce them to stay posted and to fire. The rest of the garrison notwithstanding to best of will, were not less worn down. Since the 6th, no one had gone to bed, and they were obliged to be in the works as we have said, or were employed in various indispensable labors. There remained so few men that they found neither time nor convenience for sleeping. . . .

On the 24th, we heard some firing in the direction of La Belle-Famille.[22] . . .

. . . He [an Indian scout] related the whole of our disaster, which we could scarcely believe, and we thought the English had invented the account. . . .

. . . At four o'clock, p.m., the enemy . . . sent an officer to parley, whom we admitted into the fort. He was the bearer of a letter from Johnson, who commanded the army after the death of Prideaux. . . .

This news which had first been given by the Indian, and confirmed by this officer, so broke down the courage of the garrison, that M. Pouchot and the other officers, could scarcely restrain the soldiers and militia at their posts from abandoning everything as if it were over. Had the enemy seen this disorder, they would surely have taken advantage of it. The German soldiers,[23] of whom we had many in the colonial troops, and who had come this year from France, as recruits, were more mutinous than the rest. . . .

---

[20] Canadian militiamen serving in Pouchot's forces.

[21] Openings in fortifications through which cannons were fired.

[22] Pouchot had been awaiting reinforcements from a large French and Indian force moving from Lake Erie to lift the siege. This force was destroyed by the British and their Iroquois allies at La Belle Famille on July 24.

[23] German mercenaries served in both French and British forces in North America.

13

CHRISTIAN FREDERICK POST

Delaware Indians Explain How They Fight
1758

Indians allied with British and French forces were generally loath to adopt European methods of fighting. They used flintlock muskets but not the linear formations and open-field tactics of European armies. Observers attributed this reluctance to various causes, usually blaming it on the cowardice, treachery, or insubordination of Indian warriors. Indians, of course, saw it differently. When given the opportunity, they explained clearly their way of fighting. One such occasion occurred in 1758, when the Moravian missionary Christian Frederick Post undertook a diplomatic journey from eastern Pennsylvania to the Ohio country in the company of some Delaware guides. Post knew the Delaware language well, and he recorded in his journal what the Indians told him about the differences between Native American and European methods of warfare.

There is not a prouder, or more high minded people, in themselves, than the Indians. They think themselves the wisest and prudentest men in the world; and that they can over-power both the French and English when they please. The white people are, in their eyes, nothing at all. They say, that through their conjuring craft[1] they can do what they please, and nothing can withstand them. In their way of fighting they have this method, to see that they first shoot the officers and commanders; and then, they say, we shall be sure to have them. They also say, that if their conjurers [medicine men] run through the middle of our people, no bullet can hurt them. They say too, that when they have shot the commanders, the soldiers will all be confused, and will not know what to do. They say of themselves, that every one of them is like a king and captain, and fights for himself. By this way they imagine they can

[1] Their manipulation of spiritual forces and powers.

From "The Journal of Christian Frederick Post, from Philadelphia to the Ohio, on a Message from the Government of Pennsylvania to the Delaware, Shawnese, and Mingo Indians, Settled There," in Reuben Gold Thwaites, ed., *Early Western Travels, 1748–1846* (Cleveland: A. H. Clark, 1904), 1:230–32.

overthrow any body of men, that may come against them. They say, "The English people are fools; they hold their guns half man high, and then let them snap: we take sight and have them at a shot, and so do the French; they do not only shoot with a bullet, but big swan shot."[2] They say, the French load with a bullet and six swan-shot. They further say, "We take care to have the first shot at our enemies, and then they are half dead before they begin to fight."

The Indians are a people full of jealousy, and will not easily trust any body; and they are very easily affronted, and brought into jealousy; then afterwards they will have nothing at all to do with those they suspect; and it is not brought so easy out of their minds; they keep it to their graves, and leave the seed of it in their children and grand children's minds; so, if they can, they will revenge themselves for every imagined injury. They are a very distrustful people. Through their imagination and reason they think themselves a thousand times stronger than all other people. Fort du Quesne is said to be undermined. The French have given out, that, if we overpower them, and they should die, we should certainly all die with them. When I came to the fort, the garrison, it was said, consisted of about one thousand four hundred men; and I am told they will now be full three thousand French and Indians. They are almost all Canadians, and will certainly meet the general[3] before he comes to the fort, in an ambush. You may depend upon it the French will make no open field-battle, as in the old country, but lie in ambush. The Canadians are all hunters. The Indians have agreed to draw back; but how far we may give credit to their promises the Lord knows. It is the best way to be on our guard against them, as they really could with one thousand overpower eight thousand.

---

[2] A larger size of bird shot.
[3] General John Forbes, who at this time was leading a British army west from Carlisle, Pennsylvania, to besiege Fort Duquesne.

14

PENNSYLVANIA GAZETTE

The Raid on Kittanning
1756

While professional European armies practiced siegecraft along the border between New York and Canada, warfare of a different kind engulfed the mid-Atlantic frontier. Indian and French war parties supplied out of Fort Duquesne raided frontier settlements from Pennsylvania's Lehigh Valley to Virginia's Shenandoah Valley. Colonists retaliated by mustering their militias and raising provincial forces to garrison frontier posts and pursue raiding parties. In Pennsylvania, which had no military establishment before 1755 because of its Quaker founders' pacifist principles, frontiersmen organized their own militias and adopted the tactics of la petite guerre—ambush, arson, killing of noncombatants, and mutilation of corpses—against the enemy. On September 8, 1756, three hundred Pennsylvania militiamen launched a surprise raid on Kittanning, a Delaware Indian town on the Allegheny River. As described in this newspaper account published two weeks later, the militiamen killed and scalped the town's inhabitants indiscriminately. Although they succeeded in destroying Kittanning, it was a costly victory. The militiamen suffered a high number of casualties, and on their retreat homeward, some of the captives they had recovered were recaptured.

PHILADELPHIA, SEPTEMBER 23

Saturday last arrived an Express from Colonel Armstrong,[1] Of Cumberland County, with Advice, that he marched from Fort Shirley[2] on the 30th past, with about 300 of our Provincial Forces, on an Expedition against Kittanning, a Town of our Indian Enemies, on the Ohio, about 25 Miles above Fort Duquesne. On the 3d Instant[3] he joined the Advanced

---

[1] John Armstrong commanded the first militia forces raised in Pennsylvania west of the Susquehanna River.

[2] One of several hastily constructed forts that Pennsylvania established on its frontier in 1755–1756; modern Shirleysburg, Pennsylvania.

[3] On the third day of this month—i.e., September 3.

From *Pennsylvania Gazette*, September 23, 1756.

Party at the Beaver Dams, near Franks Town;[4] and on the Seventh in the Evening, being within six Miles of Kittanning, the Scouts Discovered a Fire in the Road, and reported that there were but three, or at most four, Indians at it. It was not thought proper to attempt surprising those Indians at that Time, lest if one should escape the town might be alarmed; so Lieutenant Hogg,[5] with twelve Men, was left to watch them, with orders not to fall upon them till Day break; and our Forces turned out of the Path, to pass by their Fire without disturbing them.

About Three in the Morning, having been guided by the Whooping of the Indian Warriors at a Dance in the Town, they reached the River, 100 Perches[6] below the Body [center] of the Town, near a Corn Field, in which a Number of the Enemy lodged out of their Cabbins as it was a warm Night. As soon as Day appeared, and the Town could be seen, the Attack began in the Corn Field, through which our People charged, killing several of the Enemy, and entered the Town. Captain Jacobs,[7] Chief of the Indians, gave the War Whoop, and defended his House bravely through Loopholes in the Logs. And the Indians generally Refusing Quarter, which were offered them, declaring they were Men, and would not be Prisoners, Colonel Armstrong, (who now Received a Wound in his Shoulder by a Musket Ball) ordered their Houses to be set on Fire over their Heads, which was immediately done by the Officers and Soldiers with great Activity. When the Indians were told they would be burnt if they did not surrender, one of them reply, he did not care, as he could kill four or five before he died; and as the Heat Approached, some began to sing. Some however burst out of the Houses, and attempted to reach the River, but were instantly shot down. Captain Jacobs, in getting out of a Window, was shot and scalped, as also his Squaw, and a Lad, Called the KingSon. The Indians had a Number of spare Arms in their Houses, loaded, which went off in quick Succession as the Fire came to them; and Quantities of Gunpowder which had been stored in every House blew up from time to time, throwing some of their Bodies a great Height into the Air.

A Body of the Enemy, on the opposite Side of the River, fired on our People, and being seen to cross the River a Distance, as if to surround our Men, they [the militiamen] collected some Indian Horses that were near the Town, to carry off the Wounded, and then Retreated, without going back to the Corn Field to pick up the Scalps of those killed there

---

[4] Near modern Altoona, Pennsylvania, along an old fur-trading route.
[5] One of Armstrong's officers.
[6] An archaic unit of measurement; 100 perches equaled roughly 2,000 feet.
[7] A Delaware chief who had allied with the French.

in the Beginning of the Action. Several of the Enemy were also killed in the River as They attempted to escape by fording it: And it was computed that in all between Thirty and Forty were destroyed, though we brought off but 12 scalps. Eleven English Prisoners were released, and brought away; who informed the colonel, that besides the Powder (of which the Indians boasted they had enough for ten Years War with the English) there was a great Quantity of Goods burnt, which the French had made them a Present of but ten Days before. . . .

Captain Mercer,[8] being wounded in the action, was carted off by his Ensign and eleven Men, who left the main Body in their Return, to take another Road, and were not come in when the Express came away. He had four of the recovered Prisoners with him, and some of the Scalps. It is feared he may be intercepted.

On the Whole, it is allowed to be the greatest Blow the Indians have received since the War began, and if well followed, may soon make them weary of continuing it. The Conduct of Colonel Armstrong in marching so large a Body through the Enemy Country, and coming so close to the Town, without being discovered, is deservedly admired and applauded; and we hope their Example may have all the good Effects that are naturally to be expected from it.

[8] Another militia commander.

15

CHARLOTTE BROWN

A Woman's Perspective on Army Life
1755–1756

Eighteenth-century armies included civilians as well as soldiers. Teamsters, carpenters, and timber cutters were just some of the laborers needed to build roads and forts and move supplies between them. Women also provided essential labor to armies as nurses, cooks, and laundresses, and those who were officially attached to an army were entitled to wages, rations, and housing at its forts and encampments. Other women,

From Isabel M. Calder, ed., *Colonial Captivities, Marches and Journeys* (1935; repr., Port Washington, N.Y.: Kennikat Press, 1967), 183–88, 193–97.

typically the wives or relations of soldiers, marched with armies as "camp followers," working and living alongside the men and occasionally providing hired labor for them.

Charlotte Brown came to North America in 1755 as a civilian officer in Braddock's army. She was the matron of the military hospital, a job that put her in charge of hiring nurses and supervising the care given to the sick and wounded. A woman of genteel background, she nevertheless worked hard and endured the uncertainty and danger that went with army life. Recently widowed, she accompanied her brother, who was also attached to the army's hospital staff. During Braddock's march to Fort Duquesne, both worked in the army's hospital at Fort Cumberland on the Potomac. In 1756, Brown traveled to Albany and worked in the army hospital there. The journal she kept of her experiences illustrates the physical and psychological tribulations endured by women working for armies and the omnipresence of disease in army camps.

Daily Occurrances at Fort Cumberland

June the 14 [1755]. I was taken very ill with a Fever and other Disorders which continued 10 Days and was not able to get out of my Bed.

July the 1. My Brother was taken ill with a Fever and Flux and Fits my Maid taken ill with a Fever.

July the 4. All greatly alarm'd with the Indians scalping several Familys within 10 Miles of us one poor Boy brought in with his Scalp off he liv'd 4 Days. Several Familys left their Homes and came to the Fort for Protection.

July the 7. My Brother extremely ill he was blister'd.[1] Several who call'd themselves friendly Indians came to the Fort but the Gates were order'd to be shut they stay'd 4 Hours and then went to the Camp and we had not a drop of Water there being no Well in the Fort.

July the 8. My Brother still the same and maid very ill and I can get no Nurse so that I am very much fatigued.

July the 11. My Brother much better all of us greatly alarm'd a Boy came from the Camp and said the General was kill'd 4 Miles from the French Fort[2] and that almost all S'r Peter Hackets Regiment is cut off by a Party of French and Indians who were behind Trees. Dunbars

---

[1] An eighteenth-century medical procedure in which doctors burned the skin of a patient until it blistered, believing that doing so would draw the source of the illness out of the body via the broken skin.

[2] Brown is referring to Braddock's defeat and death a few miles from Fort Duquesne.

Regiment[3] was in the rear so that they lost but few Men it is not possible to describe the Distraction of the poor Women for their Husbands. I pack'd up my Things to send for we expected the Indians every Hour my Brother desired me to leave the Fort but I am resolv'd not to go but share my Fate with him.

July the 12. My Brother better no news from the Camp so we hope that it is not true what the Boy said.

July the 13. I am in great Distress my Brother told me if he was not better he could not live but a few Days he submitted to have Mr. Tuton one of the Dr. to attend him he gave him 2 Draughts [doses of medicine] which had a supprizing effect and I hope that he is better. An Officer is come from the Camp and confirms all what the Boy said.

July the 14. I set up with my Brother and was much suppriz'd in the Night he was so convuls'd I thought he was dying he dose'd [dozed] and I hope that he is better.

July the 15. My Brother much Better 2 Officers came from the Camp wounded and several Waggons with the Sick and some at the Point of Death.

July the 17. Oh! how shall I express my Distraction this unhappy Day at 2 in the After Noon deprived me of my dear Brother in whom I have lost my kind Guardian and Protector and am now left a friendless Exile from all that is dear to me.

July the 19. I am in so much Grief I can think of nothing Mr. Cherrington[4] was so kind as to order my Brother's funeral....

Daily Occurances at New York

. . .

April the 12 [1756]. At 3 in the Afternoon we cast Anchor at Albany all the Gentlemen went on Shore but could get no Lodging the Town being full of Officers so returned at Night.

April the 13. Went on Shore with Mr. Cherrington who was so kind as to take me a Room Went out to see the Town which is inhabited by the Dutch saw several Indians who were adorned with Beads in their Noses

---

[3] Colonel Thomas Dunbar commanded the portion of Braddock's army that had remained behind with the supply train.

[4] An officer in Braddock's army who befriended Brown.

and Ears and black Blankets being in mourning for their Friend who were kill'd in the last Campaign.[5] . . .

May the 28. 6 Men were Hanged for Desertion.

June the 1. Captain Rogers[6] came from Lake George with a french Prisoner and 1 Scalp.

June the 11. All the Town alarmed 2 Men taken by the Indians not half a Mile off.

June the 12. A Girl taken by the Indians just out of Town All the Fort Ladies came to see me.

. . .

June 16. Two Men were hang'd for Desertion. . . .

July 7. Extreamly Hot three Men dropp'd down dead as they march'd.

July 10. A Man scalp'd by the Indians on the other Side of the Water. . . .

July 19. News came that Capt. Rogers had taken eight Prisoners and four scalps. . . .

August 10. This unhappy Day I rece[iv]ed an Account of the Death of my dear Child Charlotte[7] in whom my Soul was center'd. God only knows what I suffer. when shall I die and be at rest!

August 12. All my Friends come to see me; but at present I have no Comfort in any thing. God give me Patience.

August 14. My good Friend the Minister came to see me and desired me to reconcile myself to my hard fate.

[5] Brown is describing Mohawks mourning their losses at the Battle of Lake George the previous fall.

[6] Robert Rogers, a New Englander commissioned by the British to recruit and lead rangers who would scout and fight along the Hudson-Champlain frontier.

[7] Brown had apparently left a daughter in Britain before departing for America. This is the first mention of her in Brown's journal.

16

DAVID PERRY

A New England Soldier at Ticonderoga
1758

---

*The Seven Years' War caused the largest military mobilization the North
America colonies had ever seen. In Massachusetts alone, approximately
30,000 men served in the British cause between 1755 and 1762, either
by enlisting directly in the British ranks or, more commonly, by enlisting in provincial forces raised by the colonial governments. For most of
these colonial soldiers, annual musters with their local militia units had
been the extent of their previous military experience. They recoiled from
the strict discipline, corporal punishment, and hard labor involved in
regular military service, and desertion was a constant problem for their
commanders.*

*David Perry was just sixteen years old when he served with provincial
troops from Massachusetts in a British campaign against Fort Carillon,
the French post at Ticonderoga on the southern end of Lake Champlain.
On July 8, 1758, he participated in one of the bloodiest battles of the
war, a startling defeat for the British on a par with what had happened
to General Braddock three years earlier. Commanding a force of 15,000
British regulars and provincial troops, General James Abercromby repeatedly ordered frontal assaults on the entrenchments protecting a much
smaller French force of about 3,600 men. In a memoir he wrote later in
life, Perry described the carnage he witnessed that day.*

This year [1757], in August, I was sixteen years old; at which age the
young lads of that day were called into the training-bands.[1] In the spring
of 1758, I was warned [called] to training, and there were recruiting
officers on the parade-ground, to enlist men for the next campaign. I
enlisted into Capt. Job Winslow's company, of Col. Preble's[2] regiment,

---

[1] Local militia units.
[2] Winslow and Preble were officers in the Massachusetts provincial forces.

From David Perry, *The Life of Captain David Perry, a Soldier of the French and Indian
War* (1822; repr., Tarrytown, N.Y.: William Abbatt, 1928), 8–11.

to serve eight months.—People said I would not "pass muster,"[3] as I was small of my age; but there was no difficulty about that. When the company was full we marched first to Worcester, staid there a few days, and then marched to Old Hadley. We remained here about a week. From this place we crossed the river to Northampton,[4] where we drew five days' provisions—left the place in the afternoon, and encamped a few miles out of town, in the woods for the night.—In that day there were no human habitations from Northampton, to within ten miles of Albany. . . . We had no other road than marked trees to direct our course—no bridges on which to cross the streams: some of which we waded: others we passed on trees felled by our men; and for five successive nights we lay on the ground. We arrived at Greenbush, and, after a few days' tarry, marched up the North River to a place called Setackuk,[5] where the Indians had driven off, captured, or destroyed the inhabitants. We here took a number of horses to draw the cannon to Lake George, but not having horses enough, some of the cannon were drawn by men. Part of the men went in Batteaus[6] with the provisions. When we arrived at the Lake, the army, consisting of British and Americans, amounted to about 20,000 men. It was commanded by Gen. Abrecombe, and Lord Howe[7] was second in command. We encamped there until boats and provisions enough were collected to carry us across the Lake, with cannon, etc. to attack Ticonderoga. We arrived at the Narrows the second morning after our embarkation, where we expected to be attacked by the enemy.

Major [Robert] Rogers, with his Rangers[8] was the first to land. He was joined by Lord Howe and his party, and we had proceeded but a short distance into the woods, before we were met by the enemy, and a brisk fire ensued. It was the first engagement I had ever seen, and the whistling of balls and roar of musquetry terrified me not a little. At length our regiment formed among the trees, behind which the men kept stepping from their ranks for shelter. Col. Preble, who, I well remember, was a harsh man, swore he would knock the first man down who should step out of his ranks which greatly surprised me, to think

---

[3] To be found acceptable for military service.

[4] Perry's company was marching west through Massachusetts toward Albany, New York, where a large British army was assembling to move against the French at Ticonderoga.

[5] Perry was now marching north from Albany along the Hudson River.

[6] Flat-bottomed boats used to transport troops and military supplies.

[7] George Augustus, Viscount Howe, known as Lord Howe, was a British military officer popular among the New Englanders.

[8] Rogers' Rangers served as scouts for Abercromby's army.

that I must stand still to be shot at. Pretty soon, however, they brought along some wounded Frenchmen; and when I came to see the blood run so freely, it put new life into me. The battle proved a sore one for us. Lord Howe and a number of other good men were killed.[9]

The army moved on that day to within a short distance of the enemy, and encamped for the night. In the morning we had orders to move forward again, in a column three deep, in order to storm the enemy's breastworks,[10] known in this country by the name of "the Old French Lines." Our orders were to "run to the breast-work and get in if we could." But their lines were full, and they killed our men so fast, that we could not gain it. We got behind trees, logs and stumps, and covered ourselves as we could from the enemy's fire. The ground was strewed with the dead and the dying. It happened that I got behind a white-oak stump, which was so small that I had to lay on my side, and stretch myself; the balls striking the ground within a hand's breadth of me every moment, and I could hear the men screaming, and see them dying all around me. I lay there some time. A man could not stand erect without being hit, any more than he could stand out in a shower, without having drops of rain fall upon him; for the balls come by handsfull. It was a clear day — a little air stirring. Once in a while the enemy would cease firing a minute or two, to have the smoke clear away, so that they might take better aim. In one of these intervals I sprang from my perilous situation, and gained a stand which I thought would be more secure, behind a large pine log, where several of my comrades had already taken shelter but the balls came here as thick as ever. One of the men raised his head a little above the log, and a ball struck him in the center of the forehead, and tore up his scalp clear back to the crown. He darted back, and the blood ran merrily; and rubbing his face, said it was a bad blow, and no one was disposed to deny it, for he looked bad enough. We lay there till near sunset and, not receiving orders from any officer, the men crept off, leaving all the dead, and most of the wounded. Our captain (Winslow) received a ball in his wrist, which passed up the fleshy part of his arm, and he carried it there as long as he lived, which was a number of years; he was afterwards raised to the rank of Colonel. Our Lieutenant was wounded by a shot in the leg, and one of our Sargeants received a ball in his arm, which he carried with him to his grave.

[9] Lord Howe was killed in a skirmish with the French while the British were still forming their battle lines. His loss deflated the New Englanders' enthusiasm for the campaign.

[10] As Abercromby's army moved north from Albany, the French commander at Ticonderoga, the Marquis de Montcalm, had his men construct breastworks and entrenchments that guarded the approach to the fort.

We got away the wounded of our company; but left a great many crying for help, which we were unable to afford them. I suppose that as soon as we left the ground, the enemy let loose his Indians upon them: for none of those that we left behind were heard of afterwards. We started back to our boats without any orders, and pushed out on the Lake for the night. We left between 6 and 7,000, in killed and wounded on the field of battle, which I believe is a greater number than ever was lost on our side, in one day, in all the battles that have been fought in America. We went over the Lake with about 21,000 men, in high spirits, with all kinds of music; but returned back melancholy and still, as from a funeral, and took our old stand at the south end of the Lake. . . .

Nothing of material consequence took place after this, for some time. Hardly a day passed, however, while we lay in camp, in which British and Yorkers[11] did not flog some of their men. We were employed in building a fort.

[11] New York provincial troops.

17

ROBERT ROGERS

An American Ranger Sets Down His Rules of War

1766

Robert Rogers, whose name appears in the previous two documents, was a well-known New England soldier who fought in the campaigns in the Lake Champlain region during the years 1755–1759. His commanding officers in the British army recognized his talents as a scout and commissioned him to raise his own force of colonial soldiers, known as Rogers' Rangers, who used the methods of la petite guerre *to harass the enemy. While visiting London in 1766, Rogers published his memoirs, which*

From Robert Rogers, *Journals of Major Robert Rogers: Containing an Account of the Several Excursions He Made under the Generals Who Commanded upon the Continent of North America, during the Late War* (1766; repr. Dublin: R. Acheson, 1769), 54–58, 64.

contained his rules for frontier fighting. These rules borrowed heavily from Native American precedents, and they are indicative of the ways in which Europeans adapted their military tactics to the American environment.

These volunteers I formed into a company by themselves, and took the more immediate command and management of them to myself; and for their benefit and instruction reduced into writing the following rules or plan of discipline, which, on various occasions, I had found by experience to be necessary and advantageous, viz.

I. All Rangers are to be subject to the rules and articles of war; to appear at roll-call every evening on their own parade, equipped, each with a firelock, sixty rounds of powder and ball, and a hatchet, at which time an officer from each company is to inspect the same, to see they are in order, so as to be ready on any emergency to march at a minute's warning; and before they are dismissed, the necessary guards are to be draughted [drafted], and scouts for the next day appointed.

II. Whenever you are ordered out to the enemies forts or frontiers for discoveries, if your number be small, march in a single file, keeping at such a distance from each other as to prevent one shot from killing two men, sending one man, or more, forward, and the like on each side, at the distance of twenty yards from the main body, if the ground you march over will admit of it, to give the signal to the officer of the approach of an enemy, and of their number, &c.

III. If you march over marshes or soft ground, change your position, and march abreast of each other to prevent the enemy from tracking you (as they would do if you marched in a single file) till you get over such ground, and then resume your former order, and march till it is quite dark before you encamp, which do, if possible, on a piece of ground that may afford your centries [sentries] the advantage of seeing or hearing the enemy from considerable distance, keeping one half of your whole party awake alternately through the night.

IV. Some time before you come to the place you would reconnoitre, make a stand, and send one or two men in whom you can confide, to look out the best ground for making your observations.

V. If you have the good fortune to take any prisoners, keep them separate, till they are examined, and in your return take a different route from that in which you went out, that you may the better discover any party in your rear, and have an opportunity, if their strength be superior to yours, to alter your course, or disperse, as circumstances may require.

VI. If you march in a large body of three or four hundred, with a design to attack the enemy, divide your party into three columns, each headed by a proper officer, and let those columns march in single files, the columns to the right and left keeping at twenty yards distance or more from that of the center, if the ground will admit, and let proper guards be kept in the front and rear, and suitable flanking parties at a due distance as before directed, with orders to halt on all eminences, to take a view of the surrounding ground, to prevent your being ambuscaded, and to notify the approach or retreat of the enemy, that proper dispositions may be made for attacking, defending, &c. And if the enemy approach in your front on level ground, form a front of your three columns or main body with the advanced guard, keeping out your flanking parties, as if you were marching under the command of trusty officers, to prevent the enemy from pressing hard on either of your wings, or surrounding you, which is the usual method of the savages, if their number will admit of it, and be careful likewise to support and strengthen your rear-guard.

VII. If you are obliged to receive the enemy's fire, fall, or squat down, till it is over, then rise and discharge at them. If their main body is equal to yours, extend yourselves occasionally; but if superior, be careful to support and strengthen your flanking parties, to make them equal to theirs, that if possible you may repulse them to their main body, in which case push upon them with the greatest resolution with equal force in each flank and in the center, observing to keep at due distance from each other, and advance from tree to tree, with one half of the party before the other ten or twelve yards. If the enemy push upon you, let your front fire and fall down, and then let your rear advance through them and do the like, by which time those who before were in front will be ready to discharge again, and repeat the same alternately, as occasion shall require; by this means you will keep up such a constant fire, that the enemy will not be able easily to break your order, or gain your ground. . . .

Such in general are the rules to be observed in the Ranging service; there are, however, a thousand occurrences and circumstances which may happen, that will make it necessary, in some measure, to depart from them, and to put other arts and stratagems in practice; in which cases every man's reason and judgment must be his guide, according to the particular situation and nature of things; and that he may do this to advantage, he should keep in mind a maxim never to be departed from by a commander, viz. to preserve a firmness and presence of mind on every occasion.

4

Captivity and Redemption

Captivity was a part of *la petite guerre*, the method of warfare practiced by Native Americans. When Indians went to war, they were primarily interested in acquiring people rather than land or plunder. Captives brought back home were living testimony of a war party's success and added to the captors' reputations for bravery and resourcefulness on the warpath. The war party's community also had a vested interest in acquiring captives. Some captives were communally tortured and executed, giving the community a way to vent its anger and grief over losses it had sustained in warfare. Other captives were valued for their labor and were put to work cultivating fields, processing animal pelts, or doing other jobs. Still others were adopted into Indian families; given new clothes, hairstyles, and names; and, as Indians described it, "raised up" in the place of deceased kin. In addition to these traditional motives for taking captives, Indians who became involved in European wars had another one: money. Colonial agents offered their Indian allies bounties for the captives they took, and families of captives raised funds to ransom them, relying on European and Indian intermediaries to conduct the negotiations.

Whenever the British and French went to war in North America, a new wave of captive taking occurred in the borderlands that separated Canada from British North America. During the Seven Years' War, captive taking occurred on an unprecedented scale. Approximately one thousand captives were taken by Indians along the mid-Atlantic frontier between 1755 and 1758, and probably another thousand were taken during Pontiac's War of 1763. New York and New England experienced similar crests in captive taking.

The treatment a captive received depended in large part on age and sex. Adult male captives, if not killed and scalped before the war party returned home, were likely to be marked for ritual torture and execution. Female captives, by contrast, were likely to be adopted into Indian families and eventually married to Indian husbands, with whom they would start their own families. (Unlike colonists, Indians did not stigmatize members of their society who married across racial lines, nor did they discriminate against the children of such unions.) Similarly, children would be adopted and find themselves living among new relations, all of whom regarded them as kin and contributed to their upbringing and education. They proved to be the most difficult to ransom out of captivity because the bonds of attachment forged in captivity ran both ways: Child captives were reluctant to leave their new families, and their adoptive kin grew to love them as their own.

Captives who did return to colonial society often told their stories in newspapers, short pamphlets, or books. The captivity narrative in American literature had its start in the seventeenth century among New England Puritans, who interpreted Indian captivity as a spiritual as well as a physical trial, sent by God to test the captives' worthiness for salvation. For these captives, being redeemed from captivity meant experiencing a spiritual rebirth as well as regaining their physical freedom. The Seven Years' War produced a new wave of captivity narratives from colonial presses, but many of these jettisoned the spiritual content of their New England predecessors for more lurid descriptions of Indian violence and savagery. Document 18 is a good example of such captivity narratives, which tended to demonize Indians with graphic descriptions of the depredations, tortures, and executions they inflicted on captives. Other captivity narratives, however, presented more sympathetic portrayals of Indian life. This is especially true of narratives written by captives who were adopted into Indian families. Documents 19 and 20 feature narrators whose initial impressions of Indian savagery were tempered by the kind treatment they received from their adoptive kin. As with any historical source, such narratives have their biases and limitations, but they are indispensable for studying the methods Indians used to achieve the cultural conversion of their captives.

The success Indians had in converting their captives into members of their families and communities challenged the colonists' confidence in the superiority of their way of life. European observers assumed that captives would willingly embrace the opportunity to return to their white families if given the chance, but repatriated captives often exhibited the opposite inclination, parting from their Indian kin with great reluctance and running away to rejoin them at the soonest opportunity. Document 21 describes such an occasion during Pontiac's War, when British soldiers compelled Indians to deliver up their captives en masse. When European observers conceded the superiority of Indian methods for turning strangers into kin, they undoubtedly had the experience of captives from the Seven Years' War in mind.

18

MARIE LE ROY AND BARBARA LEININGER

Two Captives from Penn's Creek
1755–1756

Marie Le Roy and Barbara Leininger immigrated to Pennsylvania from Switzerland in 1752 and Germany in 1748, respectively. They lived near each other in the frontier settlement of Penn's Creek (near modern Selinsgrove, Pennsylvania) when it was attacked by Indians in October 1755. Although their exact ages are unclear, they appear to have been teenagers at the time of their capture. They spent more than three years as captives, finally gaining their freedom after the French abandoned Fort Duquesne in late 1758. Not long afterward, their narrative was published in German in Philadelphia. In style and content, it is similar to other hastily published captivity narratives from this era.

Early in the morning of the 16th of October, 1755, while le Roy's hired man went out to fetch the cows, he heard the Indians shooting six times. Soon after, eight of them came to the house, and killed Marie le Roy's father with tomahawks. Her brother defended himself desperately, for a time, but was, at last, overpowered. The Indians did not kill him, but took him prisoner, together with Marie le Roy and a little girl, who was staying with the family. Thereupon they plundered the homestead, and set it on fire. Into this fire they laid the body of the murdered father, feet foremost, until it was half consumed. The upper half was left lying on the ground, with the two tomahawks, with which they had killed him, sticking in his head. Then they kindled another fire, not far from the house. While sitting around it, a neighbour of le Roy, named Bastian, happened to pass by on horseback. He was immediately shot down and scalped.

Two of the Indians now went to the house of Barbara Leininger, where they found her father, her brother, and her sister Regina. Her mother had gone to the mill. They demanded rum; but there was none

---

From Edmund de Schweinitz, ed., "The Narrative of Marie Le Roy and Barbara Leininger, for Three Years Captives among the Indians," *Pennsylvania Magazine of History and Biography* 29 (1905): 407–12.

in the house. Then they called for tobacco, which was given them. Having filled and smoked a pipe, they said: "We are Alleghany Indians, and your enemies. You must all die!" Thereupon they shot her father, tomahawked her brother, who was twenty years of age, took Barbara and her sister Regina prisoners, and conveyed them into the forest for about a mile. There they were soon joined by other Indians, with Marie le Roy and the little girl.

Not long after several of the Indians led the prisoners to the top of a high hill, near the two plantations [homesteads]. Toward evening the rest of the savages returned with six fresh and bloody scalps, which they threw at the feet of the poor captives, saying that they had a good hunt that day.

The next morning we were taken about two miles further into the forest, while most of the Indians again went out to kill and plunder. Toward evening they returned with nine scalps and five prisoners.

On the third day the whole band came together and divided the spoils. In addition to large quantities of provisions, they had taken fourteen horses and ten prisoners, namely: One man, one woman, five girls, and three boys. We two girls, as also two of the horses, fell to the share of an Indian named Galasko.

We traveled with our new master for two days. He was tolerably kind, and allowed us to ride all the way, while he and the rest of the Indians walked. Of this circumstance Barbara Leininger took advantage, and tried to escape. But she was almost immediately recaptured, and condemned to be burned alive. The savages gave her a French Bible, which they had taken from le Roy's house, in order that she might prepare for death; and, when she told them that she could not understand it, they gave her a German Bible. Thereupon they made a large pile of wood and set it on fire, intending to put her into the midst of it. But a young Indian begged so earnestly for her life that she was pardoned, after having promised not to attempt to escape again, and to stop her crying.

The next day the whole troop was divided into two bands, the one marching in the direction of the Ohio, the other, in which we were with Galasko, to Jenkiklamuhs,[1] a Delaware town on the West branch of the Susquehanna. There we staid ten days, and then proceeded to Puncksotonay,[2] or Eschentown. Marie le Roy's brother was forced to remain at Jenkiklamuhs.

[1] Near modern Clearfield, Pennsylvania.
[2] Modern Punxsutawney, Pennsylvania.

After having rested for five days at Puncksotonay, we took our way to Kittanny.[3] As this was to be the place of our permanent abode, we here received our welcome, according to Indian custom. It consisted of three blows each, on the back. They were, however, administered with great mercy. Indeed, we concluded that we were beaten merely in order to keep up an ancient usage, and not with the intention of injuring us. The month of December [1755] was the time of our arrival, and we remained at Kittanny until the month of September, 1756.

The Indians gave us enough to do. We had to tan leather, to make shoes (moccasins), to clear land, to plant corn, to cut down trees and build huts, to wash and cook. The want of provisions, however, caused us the greatest sufferings. During all the time that we were at Kittanny we had neither lard nor salt; and, sometimes, we were forced to live on acorns, roots, grass, and bark. There was nothing in the world to make this new sort of food palatable, excepting hunger itself.

In the month of September Col. Armstrong arrived with his men, and attacked Kittanny Town.[4] . . . We were immediately conveyed ten miles farther into the interior, in order that we might have no chance of trying, on this occasion, to escape. The savages threatened to kill us. If the English had advanced, this might have happened. For, at that time, the Indians were greatly in dread of Col. Armstrong's corps. After the English had withdrawn, we were again brought back to Kittanny, which town had been burned to the ground.

There we had the mournful opportunity of witnessing the cruel end of an English woman, who had attempted to flee out of her captivity and to return to the settlements with Col. Armstrong. Having been recaptured by the savages, and brought back to Kittanny, she was put to death in an unheard of way. First, they scalped her; next, they laid burning splinters of wood, here and there, upon her body; and then they cut off her ears and fingers, forcing them into her mouth so that she had to swallow them. Amidst such torments, this woman lived from nine o'clock in the morning until toward sunset, when a French officer took compassion on her, and put her out of her misery. An English soldier, on the contrary, named John . . . , who escaped from prison at Lancaster, and joined the French, had a piece of flesh cut from her body, and ate it. When she was dead, the Indians chopped her in two, through the middle, and let her lie until the dogs came and devoured her.

---

[3] Kittanning, a Delaware Indian town on the Allegheny.
[4] See Document 14.

Three days later an Englishman was brought in, who had, likewise, attempted to escape with Col. Armstrong, and burned alive in the same village. His torments, however, continued only about three hours; but his screams were frightful to listen to. It rained that day very hard, so that the Indians could not keep up the fire. Hence they began to discharge gunpowder into his body. At last amidst his worst pains, when the poor man called for a drink of water, they brought him melted lead, and poured it down his throat. This draught at once helped him out of the hands of the barbarians, for he died on the instant.

It is easy to imagine what an impression such fearful instances of cruelty make upon the mind of a poor captive. Does he attempt to escape from the savages, he knows in advance that if retaken, he will be roasted alive. Hence he must compare two evils, namely, either to remain among them a prisoner forever, or to die a cruel death. Is he fully resolved to endure the latter, then he may run away with a brave heart.

Soon after these occurrences we were brought to Fort Duquesne, where we remained for about two months. We worked for the French, and our Indian master drew our wages. In this place, thank God, we could again eat bread. Half a pound was given us daily. We might have had bacon, too, but we took none of it, for it was not good. In some respects we were better off than in the Indian towns; we could not, however, abide the French. They tried hard to induce us to forsake the Indians and stay with them, making us various favourable offers. But we believed that it would be better for us to remain among the Indians, in as much as they would be more likely to make peace with the English than the French, and in as much as there would be more ways open for flight in the forest than in a fort. Consequently we declined the offers of the French, and accompanied our Indian master to Sackum,[5] where we spent the winter, keeping house for the savages, who were continually on the hunt. In the spring we were taken to Kaschkaschkung,[6] an Indian town on the Beaver Creek. There we again had to clear the plantations of the Indian nobles, after the German fashion, to plant corn, and to do other hard work of every kind. We remained at this place for about one year and a half.

[5] An Indian town on the Ohio River, near modern Pittsburgh.
[6] Kuskuskies was a clustered group of four Delaware Indian communities near modern New Castle, Pennsylvania.

published postwar

A Captive's Adoption into a Seneca Family

1758

Mary Jemison was sixteen years old when she was taken captive by a French and Indian war party that attacked Scots-Irish settlers living on Marsh Creek in western Pennsylvania (near modern Chambersburg). Although she had the opportunity to return to colonial society at the end of the war, she chose to stay with her adoptive Seneca family. She married an Indian husband and eventually settled among other Senecas in the Genesee Valley in New York, where she lived through another destructive wave of European-Indian violence during the American Revolution. In 1823, she told her life story to a newspaper editor in upstate New York, who published it as A Narrative of the Life of Mrs. Mary Jemison. *She died ten years later at the age of ninety-one on the Senecas' Buffalo Creek Reservation.*

The party that took us consisted of six Indians and four Frenchmen, who immediately commenced plundering, as I just observed, and took what they considered most valuable; consisting principally of bread, meal, and meat. Having taken as much provision as they could carry, they set out with their prisoners in great haste, for fear of detection, and soon entered the woods. . . .

Mother, from the time we were taken, had manifested a great degree of fortitude, and encouraged us to support our troubles without complaining; and by her conversation seemed to make the distance and time shorter, and the way more smooth. But father lost all his ambition in the beginning of our trouble, and continued apparently lost to every care, absorbed in melancholy. . . .

As soon as I had finished my supper, an Indian took off my shoes and stockings and put a pair of moccasins on my feet, which my mother observed; and believing that they would spare my life, even if they

From James E. Seaver, ed., *A Narrative of the Life of Mrs. Mary Jemison* (1824; repr., New York: American Scenic and Historic Preservation Society, 1918), 25–40.

should destroy the other captives, addressed me as near as I can remember in the following words:

"My dear little Mary, I fear that the time has arrived when we must be parted forever. Your life, my child, I think will be spared; but we shall probably be tomahawked here in this lonesome place by the Indians. O! how can I part with you my darling? What will become of my sweet little Mary? Oh! How can I think of your being continued in captivity without a hope of your being rescued? O that death had snatched you from my embraces in your infancy; the pain of parting then would have been pleasing to what it now is; and I should have seen the end of your troubles! Alas, my dear! My heart bleeds at the thoughts of what awaits you; but, if you leave us, remember my child your own name, and the name of your father and mother. Be careful and not forget your English tongue. If you shall have an opportunity to get away from the Indians, don't try to escape; for if you do, they will find and destroy you. Don't forget, my little daughter, the prayers that I have learned you — say them often; be a good child, and God will bless you. May God bless you my child, and make you comfortable and happy." . . .

My suspicions as to the fate of my parents proved too true; for soon after I left them they were killed and scalped, together with Robert, Matthew, Betsey,[1] and the woman and her two children,[2] and mangled in the most shocking manner.[3] . . .

In the afternoon we came in sight of Fort Pitt (as it is now called),[4] where we were halted while the Indians performed some customs upon their prisoners which they deemed necessary. That fort was then occupied by the French and Indians, and was called Fort Du Quesne. It stood at the junction of the Monongahela, which is said to signify, in some of the Indian languages, the Falling-in-Banks, and the Alleghany rivers, where the Ohio river begins to take its name. The word O-hi-o, signifies bloody.

At the place where we halted, the Indians combed the hair of the young man, the boy, and myself,[5] and then painted our faces and hair red, in the finest Indian style. We were then conducted into the fort,

[1] Older siblings of Jemison, taken captive with her and her parents.

[2] Neighbors of the Jemisons, also taken captive during the raid.

[3] Mary's Indian captors told her they had to kill some of the captives they had taken because they were being pursued by soldiers and needed to move more quickly.

[4] Built by the British on the site of Fort Duquesne after it was abandoned by the French in 1758.

[5] In addition to Mary, the war party had preserved the lives of two other captives.

where we received a little bread, and were then shut up and left to tarry alone through the night. . . .

The morning at length arrived, and our masters came early and let us out of the house, and gave the young man and boy to the French, who immediately took them away. Their fate I never learned; as I have not seen or heard of them since.

I was now left alone in the fort, deprived of my former companions, and of everything that was near or dear to me but life. But it was not long before I was in some measure relieved by the appearance of two pleasant looking squaws of the Seneca tribe, who came and examined me attentively for a short time, and then went out. After a few minutes absence, they returned with my former masters, who gave me to them to dispose of as they pleased.

The Indians by whom I was taken were a party of Shawanees, if I remember right, that lived, when at home, a long distance down the Ohio.

My former Indian masters, and the two squaws, were soon ready to leave the fort, and accordingly embarked; the Indians in a large canoe, and the two squaws and myself in a small one, and went down the Ohio. . . .

Having made fast to the shore, the Squaws left me in the canoe while they went to their wigwam or house in the town, and returned with a suit of Indian clothing, all new, and very clean and nice. My clothes, though whole and good when I was taken, were now torn in pieces, so that I was almost naked. They first undressed me and threw my rags into the river; then washed me clean and dressed me in the new suit they had just brought, in complete Indian style; and then led me home and seated me in the center of their wigwam.

I had been in that situation but a few minutes, before all the Squaws in the town came in to see me. I was soon surrounded by them, and they immediately set up a most dismal howling, crying bitterly, and wringing their hands in all the agonies of grief for a deceased relative.

Their tears flowed freely, and they exhibited all the signs of real mourning. At the commencement of this scene, one of their number began, in a voice somewhat between speaking and singing, to recite some words to the following purport, and continued the recitation till the ceremony was ended; the company at the same time varying the appearance of their countenances, gestures and tone of voice, so as to correspond with the sentiments expressed by their leader:

"Oh our brother! Alas! He is dead—he has gone; he will never return! Friendless he died on the field of the slain, where his bones are yet lying unburied! Oh, who will not mourn his sad fate? No tears dropped around him; oh, no! No tears of his sisters were there! He fell in his prime, when his arm was most needed to keep us from danger! Alas! he has gone! and left us in sorrow, his loss to bewail: Oh where is his spirit? His spirit went naked, and hungry it wanders, and thirsty and wounded it groans to return! Oh helpless and wretched, our brother has gone! No blanket nor food to nourish and warm him; nor candles to light him, nor weapons of war:—Oh, none of those comforts had he! But well we remember his deeds!—The deer he could take on the chase! The panther shrunk back at the sight of his strength! His enemies fell at his feet! He was brave and courageous in war! As the fawn he was harmless: his friendship was ardent: his temper was gentle: his pity was great! Oh! our friend, our companion is dead! Our brother, our brother, alas! he is gone! But why do we grieve for his loss? In the strength of a warrior, undaunted he left us, to fight by the side of the Chiefs! His war-whoop was shrill! His rifle well aimed laid his enemies low: his tomahawk drank of their blood: and his knife flayed their scalps while yet covered with gore! And why do we mourn? Though he fell on the field of the slain, with glory he fell, and his spirit went up to the land of his fathers in war! Then why do we mourn? With transports of joy they received him, and fed him, and clothed him, and welcomed him there! Oh friends, he is happy; then dry up your tears! His spirit has seen our distress, and sent us a helper whom with pleasure we greet. Dickewamis has come: then let us receive her with joy! She is handsome and pleasant! Oh! she is our sister, and gladly we welcome her here. In the place of our brother she stands in our tribe. With care we will guard her from trouble; and may she be happy till her spirit shall leave us."

In the course of that ceremony, from mourning they became serene—joy sparkled in their countenances, and they seemed to rejoice over me as over a long lost child. I was made welcome amongst them as a sister to the two Squaws before mentioned, and was called Dickewamis; which being interpreted, signifies a pretty girl, a handsome girl, or a pleasant, good thing. That is the name by which I have ever since been called by the Indians. . . .

Being now settled and provided with a home, I was employed in nursing the children, and doing light work about the house. Occasionally I was sent out with the Indian hunters, when they went but a short distance, to help them carry their game. My situation was easy; I had no particular hardships to endure. But still, the recollection of my parents, my brothers and sisters, my home, and my own captivity, destroyed my happiness, and made me constantly solitary, lonesome, and gloomy.

My sisters would not allow me to speak English in their hearing; but remembering the charge that my dear mother gave me at the time I left her, whenever I chanced to be alone I made a business of repeating my prayer, catechism, or something I had learned in order that I might not forget my own language. By practicing in that way I retained it till I came to Genesee flats, where I soon became acquainted with English people with whom I have been almost daily in the habit of conversing.

My sisters were diligent in teaching me their language; and to their great satisfaction, I soon learned so that I could understand it readily, and speak it fluently. I was very fortunate in falling into their hands; for they were kind, good natured women; peaceable and mild in their dispositions; temperate and gentle towards me. I have great reason to respect them, though they have been dead a great number of years.

20

JAMES SMITH

Turning a Captive into an Indian
1755

James Smith was an eighteen-year-old woodcutter working for the Braddock campaign when he was taken captive near modern Bedford, Pennsylvania, in 1755. He spent five years living among the Ohio Indians before running away and returning home in 1760. He published his captivity narrative many years later, after relocating to Kentucky. His experiences bear important parallels to those of Jemison: Both were teenagers when captured, both experienced adoption into an Indian family, and both wrote about their captivity from the perspective of old age. Their narratives also offer the opportunity to compare the experiences of male and female captives, as well as those of captives who chose to return to colonial society versus those who remained with their captors.

The next morning we continued our march, and in the afternoon we came in full view of the fort [Duquesne], which stood on the point, near where Fort Pitt now stands. We then made a halt on the bank of the

From James Smith, *An Account of the Remarkable Occurrences in the Life and Travels of Col. James Smith . . . during His Captivity with the Indians, in the Years 1755, '56, '57, '58, & '59* (1799; repr., Philadelphia: Grigg, 1831), 15–18, 21–24.

Allegheny, and repeated the scalp halloo, which was answered by the firing of all the firelocks [muskets] in the hands of both Indians and French who were in and about the fort, in the aforesaid manner, and also the great guns, which were followed by the continued shouts and yells of the different savage tribes who were then collected there.

As I was at this time unacquainted with this mode of firing and yelling of the savages, I concluded that there were thousands of Indians there ready to receive General Braddock; but what added to my surprise, I saw numbers running towards me, stripped naked, excepting breechclouts [loincloths], and painted in the most hideous manner, of various colours, though the principal colour was vermilion, or a bright red; yet there was annexed to this, black, brown, blue, &c. As they approached, they formed themselves into two long ranks, about two or three rods apart. I was told by an Indian that could speak English, that I must run betwixt these ranks, and that they would flog me all the way, as I ran, and if I ran quick, it would be so much the better, as they would quit when I got to the end of the ranks. There appeared to be a general rejoicing around me, yet, I could find nothing like joy in my breast; but I started to the race with all the resolution and vigour I was capable of exerting, and found that it was as I had been told, for I was flogged the whole way. When I had got near the end of the lines, I was struck with something that appeared to me to be a stick, or the handle of a tomahawk, which caused me to fall to the ground. On my recovering my senses, I endeavoured to renew my race; but as I arose, some one cast sand in my eyes, which blinded me so, that I could not see where to run. They continued beating me most intolerably, until I was at length insensible; but before I lost my senses, I remember my wishing them to strike the fatal blow, for I thought they intended killing me, but apprehended they were too long about it. . . .

Some time after I was there, I was visited by the Delaware Indian . . . , who was at the taking of me, and could speak some English. Though he spoke but bad English, yet I found him to be a man of considerable understanding. I asked him if I had done any thing that had offended the Indians, which caused them to treat me so unmercifully? He said no, it was only an old custom the Indians had, and it was like how do you do; after that, he said, I would be well used. I asked him if I should be admitted to remain with the French? He said, no—and told me, that, as soon as I recovered, I must not only go with the Indians, but must be made an Indian myself. . . .

A few days after this the Indians demanded me, and I was obliged to go with them. I was not yet well able to march, but they took me in a canoe up the Allegheny river, to an Indian town, that was on the north side of the river, about forty miles above Fort Du Quesne. Here I remained about three weeks, and was then taken to an Indian town on the west branch of Muskingum [River]. . . .

The day after my arrival at the aforesaid town, a number of Indians collected about me, and one of them began to pull the hair out of my head. He had some ashes on a piece of bark, in which he frequently dipped his fingers, in order to take a firmer hold, and so he went on, as if he had been plucking a turkey, until he had all my hair clean out of my head, except a small spot about three or four inches square on my crown; this they cut off with a pair of scissors, excepting three locks, which they dressed up in their own mode. Two of these they wrapped round with a narrow beaded garter made by themselves for that purpose, and the other they plaited at full length, and then stuck it full of silver brooches. After this they bored my nose and ears, and fixed me off with ear-rings and nose jewels; then they ordered me to strip off my clothes and put on a breech-clout, which I did; they then painted my head, face, and body in various colours. They put a large belt of wampum on my neck, and silver bands on my hands and right arm; and so an old chief led me out in the street, and gave the alarm hallo, *coo-wigh*, several times repeated quick; and on this, all that were in the town came running and stood round the old chief, who held me by the hand in the midst. As I at that time knew nothing of their mode of adoption, and had seen them put to death all they had taken, and as I never could find that they saved a man alive at Braddock's defeat, I made no doubt but they were about putting me to death in some cruel manner.

The old chief holding me by the hand made a long speech, very loud, and when he had done, he handed me to the three young squaws, who led me by the hand down the bank, into the river, until the water was up to our middle. The squaws then made signs to me to plunge myself into the water, but I did not understand them. I thought that the result of the council was, that I should be drowned, and that these young ladies were to be the executioners. They all three laid violent hold of me, and I for some time opposed them with all my might, which occasioned loud laughter by the multitude that were on the bank of the river. At length one of the squaws made out to speak a little English (for I believe they began to be afraid of me) and said *no hurt you*; on this I gave myself up to their ladyships, who were good as their word; for though they plunged me under water, and washed and rubbed me severely, yet I could not say they hurt me much.

These young women then led me up to the council house, where some of the tribe were ready with new clothes for me. They gave me a new ruffled shirt, which I put on, also a pair of leggings done off with ribbons and beads, likewise a pair of moccasins, and garters dressed with beads, Porcupine quills, and red hair. . . . They again painted my head and face with various colours, and tied a bunch of red feathers to one of those locks they had left on the crown of my head, which stood up five or six inches. They seated me on a bearskin, and gave me a pipe, tomahawk, and polecat skin pouch, which had been skinned pocket fashion, and contained tobacco, killegenico, or dry sumach leaves, which they mix with their tobacco, also spunk, flint and steel [fire-making tools]. When I was thus seated, the Indians came in dressed and painted in their grandest manner. As they came in they took their seats, and for a considerable time there was a profound silence—every one was smoking—but not a word was spoken among them. At length one of the chiefs made a speech, which was delivered to me by an interpreter—and was as followeth: "My son, you are now flesh of our flesh, and bone of our bone. By the ceremony which was performed this day, every drop of white blood was washed out of your veins; you are taken into the Caughnewago[1] nation, and initiated into a warlike tribe; you are adopted into a great family, and now received with great seriousness and solemnity in the room and place of a great man. After what has passed this day, you are now one of us by an old strong law and custom—My son, you have now nothing to fear—we are now under the same obligations to love, support, and defend you, that we are to love and defend one another; therefore, you are to consider yourself as one of our people." At this time I did not believe this fine speech, especially that of the white blood being washed out of me; but since that time I have found that there was much sincerity in said speech, for, from that day, I never knew them to make any distinction between me and themselves in any respect whatever until I left them. If they had plenty of clothing, I had plenty; if we were scarce, we all shared one fate.

---

[1] The Caughnawagas were the descendants of Mohawks who had resettled near Montreal in the late seventeenth century. Some Caughnawagas subsequently migrated into the Ohio country in the mid-eighteenth century.

21

WILLIAM SMITH

Redeeming Captives in the Ohio Country
1764

Captives returned home in any number of ways, from escape to prisoner exchanges to ransom payments. French military officers, missionaries, and government officials often cajoled and bribed their Indian allies into giving up European captives, but they never compelled them to do so against their will. British military officers acted differently. During Pontiac's War, a military expedition led by Colonel Henry Bouquet marched into the Muskingum Valley (modern northeastern Ohio) to subdue the Delaware and Shawnee Indians living there. As part of the peace negotiations, Bouquet demanded that the Indians surrender any European captives living among them, regardless of when they were taken. The largest repatriation occurred at Bouquet's camp on the Muskingum River in November 1764 and involved more than two hundred captives. The dramatic scene of families reunited while others were torn asunder affected the British observers. William Smith, an Anglican clergyman who lived in Philadelphia, summarized their reactions in a history of the expedition he published the following year.

And here I am to enter on a scene, reserved on purpose for this place, that the thread of the foregoing narrative might not be interrupted—a scene, which language indeed can but weakly describe; and to which the Poet or Painter might have repaired to enrich their highest colorings of the variety of human passions; the Philosopher to find ample subject for his most serious reflections; and the Man to exercise all the tender and sympathetic feelings of the soul.

The scene, I mean, was the arrival of the prisoners in the camp; where were to be seen fathers and mothers recognizing and clasping their once-lost babes; husbands hanging round the necks of their newly

From [William Smith], *Historical Account of Colonel Bouquet's Expedition, against the Ohio Indians in the Year 1764* (Philadelphia: William Bradford, 1765), 26–29.

recovered wives; sisters and brothers unexpectedly meeting together after long separation, scarce able to speak the same language, or, for some time, to be sure that they were children of the same parents! In all these interviews, joy and rapture inexpressible were seen, while feelings of a very different nature were painted in the looks of others; — flying from place to place in eager enquiries after relatives not found! trembling to receive an answer to their questions! distracted with doubts, hopes, and fears, on obtaining no account of those they sought for! or stiffened into living moments of horror and woe, on learning their unhappy fate!

The Indians too, as if wholly forgetting their usual savageness, bore capital part in heightning this most affecting scene. They delivered up their beloved captives with the utmost reluctance; shed torrents of tears over them, recommending them to the care and protection of the commanding officer. Their regard to them continued all the time they remained in camp. They visited them from day to day; and brought them what corn, skins, horses and other matters, they had bestowed on them, while in their families; accompanied with other presents, and all the marks of the most sincere and tender affection. Nay, they did not stop here, but, when the army marched, some of the Indians sollicited and obtained leave to accompany their former captives all the way to Fort-Pitt, and employed themselves in hunting and bringing provisions for them on the road. A young Mingo carried this still further, and gave an instance of love which would make a figure even in romance. A young woman of Virginia was among the captives, to whom he had form'd so strong an attachment, as to call her his wife. Against all remonstrances of the imminent danger to which he exposed himself by approaching to the frontiers, he persisted in following her, at the risk of being killed by the surviving relations of many unfortunate persons, who had been captivated or scalped by those of his nation.

Those qualities in savages challenge our just esteem. They should make us charitably consider their barbarities as the effects of wrong education, and false notions of bravery and heroism; while we should look on their virtues as sure marks that nature has made them fit subjects of cultivation as well as us, and that we are called by our superior advantages to yield them all the helps we can in this way. Cruel and unmerciful as they are, by habit and long example, in war, yet whenever they come to give way to the native dictates of humanity, they exercise virtues which Christians need not blush to imitate. When they once determine to give life, they give everything with it, which, in their apprehension, belongs to it. From every enquiry that has been made, it appears—that no woman thus saved is preserved from base motives, or need fear the violation of her honor.[1] No child is otherwise treated by the persons adopting it than the children of their own body. The perpetual slavery of those captivated in war, is a notion which even their barbarity has not yet suggested to them. Every captive whom their affection, their caprice, or whatever else, leads them to live, is soon incorporated with them, and fares alike with themselves. . . .

Among the children who had been carried off young, and had long lived with the Indians, it is not to be expected that any marks of joy would appear on being restored to their parents or relatives. Having been accustomed to look upon the Indians as the only connexions they had, having been tenderly treated by them, and speaking their language, it is no wonder that they considered their new state in the light of captivity, and parted from the savages with tears.

But is must not be denied that there were even some grown persons who showed an unwillingness to return. The Shawanese were obliged to bind several of their prisoners and force them along to the camp; and some women, who had been delivered up, afterwards found means to escape and run back to the Indian towns. Some, who could not make their escape, clung to their savage acquaintance at parting, and continued many days in bitter lamentations, even refusing sustenance.

For the honor of humanity, we would suppose those persons to have been of the lowest ranks, either bred up in ignorance and distressing penury, or who had lived so long with the Indians as to forget all their former connexions. For, easy and unconstrained as the savage life is, certainly it could never be put in competition with the blessings of improved life and the light of religion, by any persons who have had the happiness of enjoying, and the capacity of discerning, them.

---

[1] In other words, Indians did not spare female captives from death so that they could sexually abuse them.

5

Diplomacy

The eighteenth-century Prussian military officer Carl von Clausewitz famously stated, "War is the continuation of politics by other means." Had he witnessed the Seven Years' War in North America, he might have substituted "diplomacy" for "politics" in that equation. Intercultural diplomacy was an art in colonial America, one that involved its own specialized rituals, tools, and vocabulary. When the diplomacy that Indians and Europeans used to make each other mutually comprehensible broke down, war broke out. Peace returned only when the diplomatic process was restored.

Long before Europeans colonized North America, Indians had developed their own customs for negotiating matters of war, peace, and trade with outsiders. Among the Iroquoian-speaking peoples of the Northeast, the condolence ritual formed the basis of this protocol. It involved speechmaking and the exchange of gifts, meant to assuage the participants' grief for their lost loved ones, so that they could renew peaceful relations with each other. The Iroquois used strings of wampum, beads manufactured from marine shells, to wipe away the tears, open the ears, and clear the throats of the aggrieved, so that they could again see, hear, and speak clearly in their councils. Among the Algonquian-speaking peoples of the Great Lakes region, the calumet ceremony served a similar purpose. Participants in diplomatic negotiations began by smoking tobacco from a long-stemmed ceremonial pipe (calumet), which dispersed ill feelings so that the mind would be open to good and productive thoughts (hence the modern English phrase "smoking the peace pipe").

European colonizers of North America had to learn these customs in order to engage successfully in diplomacy with their Indian neighbors. Their participation also changed these customs in important ways. Europeans introduced their own rituals of hospitality to the proceedings, such as toasting Indians with wine and other alcoholic beverages and firing gun salutes to them when they arrived in town. In an effort to win Indians as allies and trading partners, Europeans turned the symbolic gifts exchanged by Indians in diplomatic councils into sizable donations of material goods associated with the fur trade, such as clothing, metalware, alcohol, guns, and ammunition. When the English in 1664 conquered New Netherland (renamed New York), they inherited an alliance that the Dutch had forged with the five Iroquois nations. This became the Covenant Chain alliance that connected all of the British colonies in North America with the Indian nations affiliated with the Iroquois confederacy. By the time of the Seven Years' War, diplomacy conducted under the auspices of the Covenant Chain had become one of the chief means by which the Iroquois acquired material goods. In New France, as the French extended their fur trade into the *pays d'en haut*, intercultural diplomacy and gift giving went with it. French-allied Indians referred to the governor-general of New France as Onontio, meaning "the Great Father," who supplied them generously with gifts and helped them mediate differences and preserve peace in their country (see Document 1).

Conducting diplomacy required an expertise that few colonial officials had, and so they relied on intermediaries familiar with Indian languages and customs. These go-betweens had to be hardy souls, willing to undertake journeys that measured in the hundreds of miles, often through hostile lands. Fur traders may have seemed like a natural choice for such work, but their reputation for dishonesty gave them little credibility among Indians and colonists alike. Missionaries were more trustworthy in this regard and were often the best students of Indian languages. In a similar vein, Indian converts sometimes served as diplomatic intermediaries, as did former captives. In New France, military officers who had tours of duty in Indian country often returned to Montreal or Quebec with social connections and knowledge of Indian customs that proved useful in diplomatic negotiations.

Regardless of their background, intercultural diplomats had to possess much more than language skills. They needed to have political influence among their own people, so as to convince their audiences that they spoke with authority. They had to exhibit patience and comfort among strangers and inexhaustible generosity when hosting guests or treating friends. They also had to carry with them a highly specialized tool kit made up not just of trade goods for diplomatic presents but also of wampum beads and belts, calumets and tobacco, peace medals and other marks of distinction for powerful counterparts, and pen, ink, and paper to record their transactions. They had to be able to make persuasive speeches that employed an inventory of metaphors rooted in Native American meaning: council fires started, chains brightened, paths and roads cleared, graves covered, and hatchets buried (the source of another popular expression in modern English).

The sources in this chapter illustrate the range of diplomatic negotiations that ran concurrently with military operations during the Seven Years' War. In Document 22, a French officer new to America describes with fascination a diplomatic council between Indians from the upper Great Lakes and the governor-general of New France. In Document 23, a missionary from Pennsylvania travels far into enemy territory to convince the Ohio Indians to abandon the French as a British army marches toward Fort Duquesne. In Document 24, a Virginia military officer serves as both diplomat and hostage among the Cherokees. In Document 25, the British crown's chief Indian agent in the Northeast convenes negotiations at Fort Detroit to convince skeptical Indians that the British will ably step into the role of Onontio now that the French have surrendered Canada. In all of these source selections, we hear firsthand from the Indians themselves as they make clear their requirements for alliance and peace: generous gifts, fair trade, and security in their lands. As long as the British and French competed against each other for the Indians' goodwill, they could not afford to neglect the desires expressed by the Indians in these diplomatic encounters.

22

LOUIS-ANTOINE DE BOUGAINVILLE

French Negotiations with Indians from the Pays d'en Haut

1756

Louis-Antoine de Bougainville was a French army officer who served as aide-de-camp to General Montcalm during the Seven Years' War. He participated in the recruitment of Indians from the pays d'en haut *for the campaigns against Oswego in 1756 and Fort William Henry in 1757. Like many European military officers who were participating in*

From Edward P. Hamilton, ed., *Adventure in the Wilderness: The American Journals of Louis Antoine de Bougainville, 1756–1760* (1964; repr., Norman: University of Oklahoma Press, 1990), 8–12.

American warfare for the first time, Bougainville was simultaneously fascinated and repulsed by Indians, describing them as noble savages who possessed not only great physical beauty and dignity but also insatiable cruelty and bloodlust. He was particularly observant of the rituals and customs that regulated their diplomacy with the French, as exhibited in this journal description of negotiations between the governor-general of New France and a group of Menominees from Sinking Bay (now Green Bay, Wisconsin).

July 11 [1756]:   At noon there arrived at Montreal M. Marin,[1] a colony officer who spent the winter at the post at Sinking Bay, and who led five hundred Indians to Presque Isle,[2] the rendezvous assigned for all the Indians from the *pays d'en haut*. All have decamped, having heard it said that there was smallpox at all our forts. The Indians fear nothing so much as this disease; in fact it treats them cruelly when they are attacked by it, either because of lack of proper care, or because of a susceptibility in their blood. Only the Indians of the Menominee tribe, or the Wild Oats people, to the number of about forty, have, according to their expression, closed their eyes and risked death to come with M. Marin, first to join M. de Villiers,[3] with whom they were in the attack on the English bateaux, and afterwards to go downriver to Montreal. Wild oats are a kind of grain resembling oats, which are used just like rice and which are a very healthful form of nourishment. This plant forms the totem of this nation. The Menominees are always strongly attached to the French. They came in five great birch-bark canoes with six scalps and several prisoners.

Arrived opposite to Montreal, the canoes were placed in several lines, they lay to for some time, the Indians saluted with a discharge of guns and loud cries to which three cannon shot replied. Afterwards they came ashore and went up to the Chateau [the governor-general's house] in double file, the prisoners in the middle carrying wands decorated with feathers. These prisoners were not maltreated, as is customary upon entering into cities and villages. Entered into M. de Vaudreuil's[4] presence, the prisoners sat down on the ground in a circle and the Indian

[1] Joseph Marin de La Malgue, a French Canadian military officer.
[2] French fort on the southeastern shore of Lake Erie; modern Erie, Pennsylvania.
[3] Louis Coulon de Villiers, another French Canadian officer.
[4] The governor-general of New France, Pierre-François de Rigaud, the Marquis de Vaudreuil-Cavagnal.

chief, with action and force that surprised me, made a short enough speech, the gist of which was that the Menominees were different from the other tribes which held back part of their captures, and that they always brought back to their father all the meat they had taken.

Then they danced around the captives to the sound of a sort of tambourine placed in the middle. Extraordinary spectacle, more suited to terrify than to please; curious, however, to the eye of a philosopher who seeks to study man in conditions nearest to nature. These men were naked save for a piece of cloth in front and behind, the face and body painted, feathers on their heads, symbol and signal of war, tomahawk and spear in their hand. In general these are brawny men, large and of good appearance; almost all are very fat [cheerful]. One could not have better hearing than those people. All the movements of their body mark the cadence with great exactness. This dance is [like?] the pyrrhic [dance] of the Greeks.[5] The dance ended, they were given meat and wine. The prisoners were sent off to jail with a detachment to prevent the Algonquins and the Iroquois of the Sault[6] who were at Montreal from knocking them on the head,[7] these Indians being in mourning for the men they had lost. . . .

July 13:   The Menominees had a public audience at the Chateau during which the orator made a long harangue to M. de Vaudreuil to tell him that they alone of all his children had carried out his orders and risked the smallpox and the enemy, that the other nations had held back, perhaps as much because of not wishing to strike at the English at Oswego,[8] for whom they still held a secret inclination, as through fear of the disease. As for them, nothing could have kept them back, despite the fact that they had not been the best treated of the Indians. They complained that in a visit made [by a French agent] the previous year to carry presents to the nations of the back country they had been neglected. The answer to this speech was put off until the next day, and they were given bread and wine. On their own initiative they stationed two Indians as sentries at the Chateau door with orders to stop all Indians of their nation from entering while the General [Vaudreuil] was at table.

[5] An all-male dance accompanied by drumming described in ancient Greek texts.

[6] Algonquian and Iroquoian Indians from the *reserves* neighboring Montreal.

[7] In other words, to prevent the local Indians from killing these captives as retribution for their own losses.

[8] British fort on the southeastern shore of Lake Ontario, against which Montcalm would march in August 1756.

M. de St. Luc[9] gave them a belt of wampum in the name of the Abnakis,[10] Algonquins, and Iroquois of the Sault to exhort them to come with them to strike the English at Oswego. They accepted the belt and declared that they would come with them to partake of this meat which they had already tasted. M. de St. Luc left this evening. . . .

July 15:   . . . In the afternoon the Menominees came to hear the answer to their speech of the thirteenth and to take their leave. The answer consisted of thanks for their zeal in coming despite the smallpox, eulogies of their valor in M. de Villiers' last stroke,[11] for which those who had distinguished themselves would receive medals and gorgets,[12] word of presents which would be sent to their villages, exhortation to follow M. de Rigaud on his expedition,[13] . . . and, lastly, prayers that they should not respond to the bad advice of those who wished to destroy their obedience to their fathers' orders. To confirm these last two propositions, they were given two wampum belts which were put at the feet of the two principal chiefs.

The Menominee orator then got up, gave thanks for the presents, accepted the belts, and promised that all would follow M. de Rigaud except a few who would stay behind to take care of their wounded and sick. He asked for new canoes, for food to take them to Toronto[14] and from there to the [Green] Bay, and an outfit such as they were usually given. All these were granted to them. M. de Vaudreuil then gave two medals, one larger and the other smaller, and consequently one more honorable than the other, to two warriors, and himself put the ribbon around their necks; he also gave eight gorgets. The medals carried on one side the imprint of the King with the ordinary exergue [design], on the other a French warrior and an Indian shaking hands with these words [left blank in the manuscript]:

---

[9] Saint-Luc de La Corne, a French Canadian military officer and interpreter of Indian languages.
[10] The Abenakis were Algonquian-speaking Indians from the St. Lawrence River valley and northern New England.
[11] Villiers had recently returned from leading French and Indian war parties in western Pennsylvania.
[12] Crescent-shaped pieces of armor, usually bronze or silver, originally intended to protect the neck in battle but adapted by Indians and European military officers in North America as marks of distinction.
[13] François-Pierre de Rigaud de Vaudreuil was a French Canadian officer and the son of the governor-general. He led an advance guard that was part of the French assault on Oswego in August 1756.
[14] French post on the northern shore of Lake Ontario.

This ceremony accomplished, M. Marin, gathering up the belts, sang the war song for M. de Vaudreuil, the Indians keeping time with a guttural inhalation. Then he gave the belts back to the two first chiefs, who had also sung their war songs one after the other. A third sang after them, the assembly was over, and the Indians withdrew, carrying away the scalps, the wands decorated with feathers, a kind of trophy, and the banners they had stored with M. de Vaudreuil. They will be outfitted tomorrow and will leave the next day under the leadership of M. Marin.

23

CHRISTIAN FREDERICK POST

A Missionary Conducts Diplomacy in the Ohio Country
1758

Christian Frederick Post was a German Moravian missionary whose residence among Delaware Indian converts had familiarized him with their customs and language. In the summer of 1758, he undertook a diplomatic mission for the Pennsylvania government, traveling west from Philadelphia with a small party of Delaware Indians to convince the Ohio Indians to stand aside as a British army commanded by General John Forbes marched toward Fort Duquesne. In his journal, Post recorded his negotiations with these Indians, many of whom were still allied with the French.

[August] 26th [1758].—The Indians, with a great man of the French officers, came over to hear what I had to say. The officers brought with them a table, pens, ink and paper.[1] I spoke in the middle of them with

---

[1] Post was addressing French-allied Indians camped outside Fort Duquesne.

From "The Journal of Christian Frederick Post, from Philadelphia to the Ohio, on a Message from the Government of Pennsylvania to the Delaware, Shawnese, and Mingo Indians, Settled There," in Reuben Gold Thwaites, ed., *Early Western Travels, 1748–1846* (Cleveland: A. H. Clark, 1904), 1:204, 206–9, 213–16.

a free conscience, and perceived by the look of the French, they were not pleased with what I said; the particulars of which were as follows; I spoke in the name of the government and people of Pensilvania.

"Brethren at Allegheny, We have a long time desired to see and hear from you; you know the road was quite stopt; and we did not know how to come through. We had sent many messengers to you; but we did not hear of you; now we are very glad we have found an opening to come and see you, and to speak with you, and to hear your true mind and resolution. We salute you very heartily."   A string, No. 1.[2]

. . .

"Hearken, brethren at Allegheny. I have told you that we really made peace with part of your nation, twelve months past; I now by this belt open the road from Allegheny to our council fire, where your grandfathers kept good councils with us, that all may pass without molestation or danger. You must be sensible, that unless a road be kept open, people at variance can never come together to make up their differences. Messengers are free in all nations throughout the world, by a particular token. Now, brethren at Allegheny, I desire you will join with me in keeping the road open, and let us know in what manner we may come free to you, and what the token shall be. I join both my hands to yours, and will do all in my power to keep the road open."   A belt of seven rows.[3]

"Now, brethren at Allegheny, Hear what I say. Every one that lays hold of this belt of peace, I proclaim peace to them from the English nation, and let you know that the great king of England does not incline to have war with the Indians; but he wants to live in peace and love with them, if they will lay down the hatchet, and leave off war against him.

"We love you farther, we let you know that the great king of England has sent a great number of warriors into this country, not to go to war against the Indians, in their towns, no, not at all; these warriors are going against the French; they are on the march to the Ohio, to revenge the blood they have shed. And by this belt I take you by the hand, and lead you at a distance from the French, for your own safety, that your legs may not be stained with blood. Come away on this side of the mountain,[4] where we may oftener converse together, and where your own flesh and blood lives. We look upon you as our countrymen, that sprung out of the same ground with us; we think, therefore, that it is our duty to take care of you, and we in brotherly love advise you to come away with your

---

[2] A string of wampum, the first Post gave during this speech.
[3] A wampum belt made of seven strings of wampum beads woven together.
[4] In other words, relocate east of the Allegheny Mountains, away from the French.

whole nation, and as many of your friends as you can get to follow you. We do not come to hurt you, we love you, therefore we do not call you to war, that you may be slain; what benefit will it be to you to go to war with your own flesh and blood? We wish you may live without fear or danger with your women and children." The large peace belt.

. . .

"Brethren, One thing I must bring to your remembrance. You know, if any body loses a little child, or some body takes it from him, he cannot be easy, he will think on his child by day and night; since our flesh and blood is in captivity, in the Indian towns, we desire you will rejoice the country's heart, and bring them to me; I shall stretch out my arms to receive you kindly." A string.

After I had done, I left my belts and strings still before them. The Delawares[5] took them all up, and laid them before the Mingoes;[6] upon which they rose up, and spoke as follows:

"Chau [Post], What I have heard pleases me well; I do not know why I go to war against the English. Noques [Mingoes?], what do you think? You must be strong. I did not begin the war, therefore, I have little to say; but whatever you agree to, I will do the same." Then he addressed himself to the Shawanese, and said, "You brought the hatchet to us from the French, and persuaded us to strike our brothers the English; you may consider (laying the belts, &c. before them) wherefore you have done this."

The Shawanese acknowledged they received the hatchet from the French, who persuaded them to strike the English; that they would now send the belts to all the Indians, and in twelve days would meet again.

Present at this council, three hundred French and Indians. They all took leave, and went over again to the fort [Duquesne], but my companions, who were about seventy in number.

Shamokin Daniel,[7] who came with me, went over to the fort by himself, (which my companions disapproved of) and counseled with the Governor;[8] who presented him with a laced coat and hat, a blanket, shirts, ribbons, a new gun, powder, lead, &c. When he returned he was quite changed, and said, "See here, you fools, what the French have given me. I was in Philadelphia, and never received a farthing"; and,

---

[5] The Ohio Delawares were generally more inclined to accept Post's peace overtures than other Indians in the Forks of the Ohio region.

[6] Iroquois, primarily Senecas, living in the Ohio country.

[7] A Delaware Indian from the Susquehanna Valley who had joined Post's party as it traveled west.

[8] François-Marie Le Marchand de Lignery, the French commander at the fort.

directing himself to me, he said, "The English are fools, and so are you."
In short, he behaved in a very proud, saucy and imperious manner. He
further said, "The English never give the Indians any powder, and that
the French would have given him a horseload, if he would have taken it;
see that young man there, he was in Philadelphia and never got any thing;
I will take him over to the French; and get some cloathing for him."

. . .

September 1st [Kuskuskies].[9]—Shingas, King Beaver, Delaware
George, and Pisquetumen, with several other captains[10] said to me,

"Brother, We have thought a great deal since God has brought you to
us; and this is a matter of great consequence, which we cannot readily
answer; we think on it, and will answer you as soon as we can. Our feast
hinders us; all our young men, women and children are glad to see you;
before you came, they all agreed together to go and join the French;
but since they have seen you, they all draw back; though we have great
reason to believe you intend to drive us away, and settle the country; or
else, why do you come to fight in the land that God has given us?"

I said, we did not intend to take the land from them; but only to
drive the French away. They said, they knew better; for that they were
informed so by our greatest traders; and some Justice of the Peace had
told them the same, and the French, said they, tell us much the same
thing, "that the English intend to destroy us, and take our lands"; but
the land is ours, and not theirs; therefore, we say, if you will be at peace
with us, we will send the French home. It is you that have begun the
war, and it is necessary that you hold fast, and be not discouraged, in the
work of peace. We love you more than you love us; for when we take any
prisoners from you, we treat them as our own children. We are poor, and
yet we clothe them as well as we can, though you see our children are
as naked as at the first.[11] By this you may see that our hearts are better
than yours. It is plain that you white people are the cause of this war;
why do not you and the French fight in the old country, and on the sea?
Why do you come to fight on our land? This makes every body believe,
you want to take the land from us by force, and settle it.

. . .

[9] After meeting with the Indians near Fort Duquesne, Post moved to Kuskuskies, a
group of Delaware towns on Beaver Creek, where he received a warmer reception.
[10] Shingas (see Document 11), King Beaver (also known as Tamaqua), Delaware
George, and Pisquetomen were all Delaware chiefs.
[11] In other words, as naked as when they were born.

They said, "Brother, your heart is good, you speak always sincerely; but we know there are always a great number of people that want to get rich; they never have enough; look, we do not want to be rich, and take away that which others have. God has given you the tame creatures; we do not want to take them from you. God has given to us the deer, and other wild creatures, which we must feed on; and we rejoice in that which springs out of the ground, and thank God for it. Look now, my brother, the white people think we have no brains in our heads; but that they are great and big, and that makes them make war with us: we are but a little handful to what you are; but remember, when you look for a wild turkey you cannot always find it, it is so little it hides itself under the bushes: and when you hunt for a rattlesnake, you cannot find it; and perhaps it will bite you before you see it. However, since you are so great and big, and we so little, do you use your greatness and strength in compleating this work of peace. This is the first time that we saw or heard of you, since the war begun, and we have great reason to think about it, since such a great body of you come into our lands.[12] It is told us, that you and the French contrived the war, to waste the Indians between you; and that you and the French intended to divide the land between you. . . ."

Then I said, "Brothers, I am very sorry to see you so jealous. I am your own flesh and blood, and sooner than I would tell you any story that would be of hurt to you, or your children, I would suffer death: and if I did not know that it was the desire of the Governor, that we should renew our old brotherly love and friendship, that subsisted between our grandfathers, I would not have undertaken this journey. I do assure you of mine and the people's honesty. If the French had not been here, the English would not have come, and consider, brothers, whether, in such a case, we can always sit still."

Then they said, "It is a thousand pities we did not know this sooner; if we had, it would have been peace long before now."

---

[12] Forbes's army, which was then making its way toward Fort Duquesne.

24

HENRY TIMBERLAKE

A Virginia Military Officer Serves as a Diplomat and Hostage among the Cherokees

1761

Henry Timberlake was a Virginia military officer who, like his contempo-
rary George Washington, hoped to distinguish himself in the king's service
and thereby secure a commission in the British army. For that reason,
he volunteered for a dangerous assignment during the Cherokee War of
1759–1761. At the request of the Cherokees, Timberlake agreed in late
1761 to travel to the Overhill Cherokee towns (a branch of the nation liv-
ing in what is now eastern Tennessee) to spread news of the peace terms
that had been negotiated between the British and Cherokees. Although his
mission was primarily diplomatic, Timberlake was interested in map-
ping a route into Cherokee country should the British decide to attack the
Overhill towns. He was also serving as a hostage, as his Indian protectors
expected that his presence in the remote Overhill country would discour-
age the British from breaking the peace. It is worthwhile to compare
Timberlake's description of his experience with that of Louis-Antoine de
Bougainville (see Document 22); both were military officers who found
themselves unexpectedly engaged in Native American diplomatic rituals.

We were received at Tommotly[1] in a very kind manner by Ostenaco,[2]
the commander in chief. . . .

   After smoaking and talking some time, I delivered a letter from Colonel Stephen,[3] and another from Captain M'Neil,[4] with some presents
from each, which were gratefully accepted by Ostenaco and his consort.

---

[1] One of the Overhill towns.
[2] One of the Overhill chiefs, who favored alliance with the British. This meeting
between Ostenaco and Timberlake initiated a diplomatic partnership that eventually
brought both men to London for an audience with King George II in 1762.
[3] Colonel Adam Stephen had authorized Timberlake's trip.
[4] Another one of Timberlake's superior officers.

From Henry Timberlake, *The Memoirs of Lieut. Henry Timberlake* (London: J. Ridley and
C. Henderson, 1765), 30–39.

He gave me a general invitation to his house, while I resided in the country; and my companions[5] found no difficulty in getting the same entertainment, among an hospitable, tho' savage people, who always pay a great regard to anyone taken notice of by their chiefs.

Some days after, the headmen of each town were assembled in the town-house of Chote,[6] the metropolis of the country, to hear the articles of peace read, whither the interpreter and I accompanied Ostenaco.

The town-house, in which are transacted all public business and diversions, is raised with wood, and covered over with earth, and has all the appearance of a small mountain at a little distance. It is built in the form of a sugar loaf, and large enough to contain 500 persons, but extremely dark, having, besides the door, which is so narrow that but one at a time can pass, and that after much winding and turning, but one small aperture to let the smoak out, which is so ill contrived, that most of it settles in the roof of the house. Within it has the appearance of an ancient amphitheatre, the seats being raised one above another, leaving an area in the middle, in the center of which stands the fire; the seats of the head warriors are nearest it.

They all seemed highly satisfied with the articles. The peace-pipe was smoaked, and Ostenaco made an harangue [speech] to the following effect:

"The bloody tommahawke, so long lifted against our brethren the English, must now be buried deep, deep in the ground, never to be raised again; and whoever shall act contrary to any of these articles, must expect a punishment equal to his offence. Should a strict observance of them be neglected, a war must necessarily follow, and a second peace may not be so easily obtained. I therefore once more recommend to you, to take particular care of your behaviour towards the English, whom we must now look upon as ourselves; they have the French and Spaniards to fight, and we enough of our own colour, without medling with either nation. I desire likewise, that the white warrior, who has ventured himself here with us, may be well used and respected by all, wherever he goes amongst us."

The harangue being finished, several pipes were presented to me by the headsmen, to take a whiff. This ceremony I could have waved, as smoaking was always very disagreeable to me; but as it was a token of

---

[5] Timberlake traveled with a small party that included another soldier and an interpreter.

[6] Chota was the chief town in the Overhill country and the seat of its diplomacy with outsiders.

their amity, and they might be offended if I did not comply, I put on the best face I was able, though I dared not even wipe the end of the pipe that came out of their mouths; which, considering their paint and dirtiness, are not the most ragoutant, as the French term it.[7]

After smoaking, the eatables were produced, consisting chiefly of wild meat; such as venison, bear, and buffalo; tho' I cannot much commend their cookery, every thing being greatly overdone: there were likewise potatoes, pumpkins, homminy, boiled corn, beans, and pease, served up in small flat baskets, made of split canes, which were distributed amongst the croud; and water, which, except the spirituous liquor brought by the Europeans, is their only drink, was handed about in small goards. What contributed greatly to render this feast disgusting, was eating without knives and forks, and being obliged to grope from dish to dish in the dark. After the feast there was a dance, but I was already so fatigued with the ceremonies I had gone through, that I retired to Kanagatucko's hot-house;[8] but was prevented taking any repose by the smoke, with which I was almost suffocated, and the croud of Indians that came and sat on the bedside; which indeed was not much calculated for repose to any but Indians, or those that had passed an apprenticeship to their ways, as I had done: it was composed of a few boards, spread with bear skins, without any other covering; the house being so hot, that I could not endure the weight of my own blanket.

Some hours after I got up to go away, but met Ostenaco, followed by two or three Indians, with an invitation from the headman of Settico,[9] to visit him the next day.

I set out with Ostenaco and my interpreter in the morning, and marched towards Settico, till we were met by a messenger, about half a mile from the town, who came to stop us till every thing was prepared for our reception: from this place I could take a view of the town where I observed two stand of colours flying,[10] one at the top, and the other at the door of the town-house; they were as large as a sheet, and white. Lest therefore I should take them for French, they took great care to inform me, that their custom was to hoist red colours as an emblem of war; but white, as a token of peace. By this time we were joined by another messenger, who desired us to move forward.

---

[7] In other words, Timberlake found the Indians' pipes dirty and unappetizing.
[8] Kanagatucko was a Cherokee chief known as "Old Hop" among the British. Timberlake is describing a sweat lodge attached to the chief's dwelling.
[9] Another Overhill town.
[10] Two flags or banners.

About 100 yards from the townhouse we were received by a body of between three and four hundred Indians, ten or twelve of which were entirely naked, except a piece of cloth about their middle, and painted all over in a hideous manner, six of them with eagle tails in their hands, which they shook and flourished as they advanced, danced in a very uncommon figure, singing in concert with some drums of their own make . . . with several other instruments, uncouth beyond description. Cheulah, the headman of the town, led the procession, painted blood-red, except his face, which was half-black, holding an old rusty broadsword in his right hand, and an eagle's tail in his left. As they approached, Cheulah, singling himself out from the rest, cut two or three capers [frantic dances], as a signal to the other eagle-tails, who instantly followed his example. This violent exercise, accompanied by the band of musick, and a loud yell from the mob, lasted about a minute, when the headman waving his sword over my head, struck it into the ground, about two inches from my left foot; then directing himself to me, made a short discourse (which my interpreter told me was only to bid me a hearty welcome) and presented me with a string of beads. We then proceeded to the door, where Cheulah, and one of the beloved men [chiefs], taking me by each arm, led me in, and seated me in one of the first seats; it was so dark that nothing was perceptible till a fresh supply of canes were brought, which being burnt in the middle of the house answers both purposes of fuel and candle. I then discovered about five hundred faces; and Cheulah addressing me a second time, made a speech much to the same effect as the former, congratulating me on my safe arrival thro' the numerous parties of the northern Indians, that generally haunt the way I came. He then made some professions of friendship, concluding with giving me another string of beads, as a token of it. He had scarce finished, when four of those who had exhibited at the procession made their second appearance, painted milk-white, their eagle-tails in one hand and small goards with beads in them in the other, which they rattled in time to the musick. During this dance the peace-pipe was prepared; the bowl of it was of red stone, curiously cut with a knife, it being very soft, tho' extremely pretty when polished. Some of these are of black stone, and some of the same earth they make their pots with, but beautifully diversified. The stem is about three feet long, finely adorned with porcupine quills, dyed feathers, deers hair, and such like gaudy trifles.

After I had performed my part with this, I was almost suffocated with the pipes presented me on every hand, which I dared not decline. They might amount to about 170 or 180, which made me so sick, that I could not stir for several hours.

25

WILLIAM JOHNSON

A British Diplomat Extends the Covenant Chain Westward

1761

The British crown appointed Sir William Johnson its superintendent of Indian affairs in the northern colonies in 1756. During the Seven Years' War, his home in New York's Mohawk Valley replaced Albany as the "council fire" for the Covenant Chain alliance between the Iroquois confederacy and the British colonies. After the conquest of Canada in 1760, Johnson also became responsible for conducting the crown's diplomacy with Indians in the pays d'en haut *who were formerly allied with the French. In the summer of 1761, Johnson undertook a major diplomatic embassy to extend the Covenant Chain alliance to these Indians. In a treaty conference at Fort Detroit, he sought to restore peace with these nations. As indicated in the conference minutes excerpted here, the Indians present also expressed their concerns about the British.*

[Detroit, September 9, 1761]

Sir William opened the Conference with the following Speech —

Brethren of the several Nations here assembled,[1] Sachems [distinguished chiefs], Chieftains & Warriors —

It gives me great pleasure to meet so many Nations assembled here on my summons, and as I come a long journey to see, and talk with you, on matters relative to our interest, in order to prepare you to hear the same I do agreeable to the Custom of our Ancestors, wipe away those Tears from your Eyes which were shed for the losses you sustained during the War in which you were imprudently engaged against the En-

---

[1] Johnson was addressing delegations from several Indian nations living in the upper Great Lakes region, including Wyandots, Kickapoos, Ojibwas, Ottawas, Miamis, and Potawatomis.

From *Papers of Sir William Johnson*, ed. James Sullivan, Alexander C. Flick, Milton W. Hamilton, and Albert B. Corey (Albany: University of the State of New York, 1921), 3:475–79, 483, 485–87.

glish, that you may clearly discern your present interest & look with a Chearfull and friendly countenance when you speak with, or are spoke to by your brethren the English.

Gave three Strings of Wampum

Brethren

Having cleared your Sight, I do in the next place open the passage to your heart that you may at this Meeting speak honestly & brotherlike, & not from the Lips as some unthinking and evil minded Nations have lately done—

Gave three Strings

Brethren

Several of our people being killed in the War in which you were engaged against us. I now therefore wipe away the blood which was shed that the sight thereof may no more offend or grieve you—

Gave three Strings

Brethren

I do also pluck out of your heads the Hatchet with which we were obliged to strike you, & apply a healing salve to the Wound.

Gave a belt of 7 Rows

Brethren

As the bones of those people which you have lost, do now require interment, I do with this belt of Wampum gather them all together, bury them deep, & level the graves with the ground so that they may no more be seen—

Gave a black Belt[2] of 15 Rows

Brethren

The great King George my Master being graciously pleased some years ago to appoint me to the Sole management & Care of all his Indian Allies in the Northern parts of North America directed me to light up a large Council fire at my House in the Mohocks Country for all Nations of Indians in amity with his Subjects, or who were inclined to put themselves under his Royal protection to come thereto, and receive the benefit thereof. This fire yields such a friendly warmth that many Nations have since assembled thereto, and daily partake of its influence—I have therefore now brought a brand thereof with me to the place with which I here kindle up a large Council fire made of such Wood as shall burn bright & be unextinguishable, whose kindly Warmth shall be felt in, and

---

[2] "Black" wampum was made out of purple wampum beads and was often used as a condolence gift.

shall extend to the most remote Nations, and shall induce all Indians, even from the setting of the Sun to come hither and partake thereof—

Gave a belt of nine Rows

. . .

Brethren

With this belt In the name of his Britannick Majesty I strengthen and renew the antient Covenant Chain formerly subsisting between us, that it may remain bright & lasting to the latest Ages, earnestly recommending it to you, to do the same, and to hold fast thereby as the only means by which you may expect to become a happy & flourishing people.

Gave a belt of the Covenant Chain[3] containing 20 Rows of Wampum

. . .

Brethren

I can with confidence assure you that it is not at present, neither hath it been his Majestys intentions to deprive any Nation of Indians of their Just property by taking possession of any Lands to which they have a lawfull Claim, farther than for the better promoting of an extensive Commerce, for the security and protection of which (and for the occupying of such posts as have been surrendered to us by the Capitulation of Canada) Troops are now on their way; I therefore expect that you will consider and treat them as Brethren, and continue to live on terms of the strictest Friendship with them—and as I now declare these his Majestys favourable intentions to do you justice, I expect in return that nothing shall on your parts be wanting to testify the just Sense which you all conceive of his Majesty's favour, and of your earnest desire to live with the British Subjects on the terms of friendship and alliance—

Gave a belt of 7 Rows

Brethren

I have heard with great satisfaction from Mr. Croghan[4] that agreeable to my desire made to the several Nations two years Ago, of delivering up what English prisoners remained amongst you, or were still in your possession, you have in Consequence thereof given up a Considerable number and as we are now to be united by Alliance & become one

---

[3] Covenant Chain belts were generally large belts used to renew the multilateral Covenant Chain alliance.

[4] George Croghan was a Pennsylvania fur trader who served as a deputy Indian commissioner for Johnson.

people, I expect you will likewise discharge any who yet remain with you—Agreable to the promises then made—

Gave a belt of 7 Rows

Brethren

It gives me great concern to hear daily complaints from your Brethren the English against you on account of your stealing his Majestys Horses, & those of the Traders who bring goods to dispose of amongst you; As a behaviour of this kind so unlike that of Brethren may, if not imediately discontinued be productive of very fatal Consequences—I therefore by this belt recommend it to you all to desist for the future from a practice so mean, & scandalous & unbecoming the Character of Men who claim the title of Brethren and British Allies, and I hope that what I have now been obliged to say on that head will sufficiently put a Stop thereto & prevent me from being obliged to consider you as a people incapable of relishing the benefit of friendly admonition or advice—

Gave a belt of 8 Rows

. . .

[September 10, 1761]

P. M.   The Indians all assembled to deliver in their Answer Present as Yesterday

Anáiása, Chief of the Hurons, addressed Sir William as follows

Brother Warraghiyagey[5]

By this Belt we return you our Sincerest acknowledgments for your compliance with the Customs of our forefathers in drying up those tears which were shed for our losses in the War which we were imprudently led into against the English, as also for clearing our sight so that we may now see our interest—

Brother

We return you hearty thanks for your goodness in clearing and opening the passage to our hearts, so as to enable us to speak our Mind freely together, and we are greatly rejoiced and return [thanks] to the great being above, for preserving and conducting you hither for so good a purpose which we are certain must afford great satisfaction to all Indians whatsoever—

A belt

. . .

[5] Johnson's Indian name, roughly translated as "Doer of Great Things."

Brother

We thank you for renewing the old Covenant Chain subsisting between our Ancestors & you, and we on our parts heartily concur with you therein, and with this belt we now renew & strengthen it, and shall hold fast by it for ever—

A belt

... We therefore with pleasure embrace This union, and we joyn ourselves together with our Brethren with a strong Chain which can never be broken, and we hope that on your parts you will do the same, and that you will never forget the Words which you have now made use of, but that you will send us a plenty of goods, & that at a Cheaper rate than we have hitherto been able to procure them—

A belt

Brother

It gives us great satisfaction to hear that the King has no intentions to deprive us of our Lands (of which we were once very apprehensive) and as to the Troops who are now going to the distant posts, we are well pleased therewith, and hope they will look upon and treat us as Brethren, in which light they shall always be Esteemed by us as we are determined to live on the best terms with them—

A belt

Brother

We are greatly concerned to find you have had any occasion to speak to us concerning the stealing of horses, which, be assured has never been done with either our approbation or Consent, but has proceeded from some of our idle young Men who you know are very difficult to restrain, however, we shall for the future exert ourselves & do all in our power to put a stop to that, or any thing else which may give you uneasiness, and we believe that what you have sayed thereon at this Meeting will make them ashamed, & prevent their so doing for the future—

A belt

Brother

You have spoke to us concerning the English prisoners—which we delivered up, & desired if any remained yet amongst us that we might imediately set them free— ... But we must observe that they are no Slaves with us, being at their free liberty to go anywhere, or act as they please, neither is it our Custom to Exercise any Authority over them, they having the same priviledges with ourselves—We beg you will not suppose that we ever [ill treated] any, or detained them a moment longer than they chose to stay, and now assure you that we have not one remaining amongst us, having delivered over Six, which were the last we had, to Mr. Croghan some days ago—

A belt

Brother

Many of our people having been frequently ill used as well by the Soldiers, as Inhabitants of this place, we therefore entreat you to take the same into your consideration & prevent them from so doing for the future—

There is but one thing more which we have to say to you before we Make an end, that is, to remind you of your promises concerning trade, of which, and of the dearness of goods, and Scarcity of ammunition we could say a great deal, The traders selling their Goods so dear that we are scarcely able to purchase them, besides, many articles are very scarce & in particular powder is sold so sparingly & is so hard to be got that we are all apprehensive we must shortly be obliged to leave off hunting entirely, as our Young Men cannot procure sufficient to cloath themselves or provide for their Wives & Children; all which Brother we beg you will seriously consider on & let us have our goods cheaper & a sufficiency of powder for our hunting so that we may be enabled to trade as formerly.—

A belt

6

Savagery and Civility

Many events associated with the Seven Years' War in North America have been described as "raids" or "massacres."* These events may be distinguished from "battles" in that they did not involve professional soldiers fighting according to the conventional rules of European warfare. Instead, raids and massacres were carried out by irregular forces — militiamen, rangers, vigilantes, or Indians — often against civilians or unarmed opponents.

Another distinction affected how raids and massacres made it into the history books. Generally speaking, when Indians conducted such hostilities, they were described for posterity as massacres. In the Oswego Massacre (1756) and the Fort William Henry Massacre (1757), French-allied Indians attacked soldiers and civilians who had already surrendered. In the massacres at Great Cove (1755; see Document 11) and Fort Granville (1756), Indian war parties attacked settler communities in western Pennsylvania. In contrast, attacks by colonial forces on Indian towns have been labeled as raids, such as the raid on Kittanning in 1756 (see Document 14) and the raid on Saint-François, an Abenaki Indian town in the St. Lawrence River valley, in 1759. John Armstrong and Robert Rogers, the leaders of the Kittanning and Saint-François raids, respectively, were lauded as heroes by their contemporaries, despite their use of the same tactics — surprise attacks, killing of unarmed civilians, scalping and other mutilation of corpses — that characterized Indian "massacres."

As you might suspect, the distinction between a raid and a massacre had little to do with the tactics involved and much more to do with who employed them. European observers described the Indians' methods of warfare as outward expressions of their innate savagery. Indians, they believed, fought by ambush and surprise because they were cowardly and unwilling to face armed soldiers in open combat. Likewise, they tortured captives because of their inherent bloodlust, and they mutilated corpses and cannibalized the dead because their basest human instincts had not yet been curbed by Christian civilization. Professional soldiers who came to North America to fight the Seven Years' War claimed to practice civilized warfare because they fought according to a shared set of rules aimed at confining violence to uniformed combatants and treating defeated enemies with magnanimity. European military officers also considered themselves bound by aristocratic standards of gentility and generosity that transcended national borders. Yet they believed that the rules of civilized warfare could be legitimately suspended against certain kinds of enemies, such as rebels, non-Christians, or those who refused to fight by the same standards.

No matter how much Europeans insisted on drawing this line between savagery and civility, the nature of combat in North America blurred it. European officers and soldiers came face-to-face not only with Native Americans but also with colonial militias and irregular forces that adopted Indian methods of warfare without hesitation or moral qualms. British and French army officers described Indian allies as unreliable and unmanageable, but neither side was willing to dispense with them for fear that doing so would benefit the enemy. Nor were they willing to interfere with the Indians' methods of fighting for fear that they would lose their cooperation. In the same manner, European officers condemned the insubordination and poor training of colonial soldiers, but they readily recruited and supplied them for service as irregulars, dispatching them to terrorize enemy Indian and colonial civilians and rewarding them with plunder and bounties when they succeeded. Colonists clamored for their governments to authorize scalp bounties, a measure that essentially endorsed vigilantism against Indians, regardless of their wartime alliances.

During the Seven Years' War, an unprecedented level of intercultural violence erupted in colonial America. In newspapers, captivity narratives, pamphlets, and private correspondence, writers used racial language to reinforce the difference between savagery and civility. When both sides murdered noncombatants and scalped the dead, tactics alone no longer explained who prosecuted war justly and who did not. Instead, to justify their own embrace of such methods, Europeans resorted to describing Indians as biologically and irredeemably corrupt, fit only for eradication from the face of the earth. This rhetoric anticipated the forced removal and widespread dispossession of native peoples that accompanied American westward expansion in the nineteenth century.

The sources in this chapter explore the tension between savagery and civility by looking at three incidents that involved breaking the rules of what Europeans considered to be civilized warfare. Document 26 offers a French eyewitness account of the Fort William Henry

Massacre, when Indians attacked an unarmed British garrison after it had negotiated a surrender to the French. Document 27 offers another version of that event, this one from the famous American novel *The Last of the Mohicans*, written more than sixty years later. Document 28 concerns the Fort Pitt incident, when officers in the British army discussed using smallpox as a biological weapon against Indians involved in Pontiac's War. Documents 29 and 30 reflect the debate generated in the colonial press by the notorious Paxton Boys, frontier vigilantes who murdered the entire population of a small Indian town in 1763.

26

PIERRE ROUBAUD

A French View of the Fort William Henry Massacre

1757

Pierre Roubaud was a Jesuit missionary at Saint-François, an Abenaki town northeast of Montreal in the St. Lawrence River valley (see Map 1, page 2). As was common among the French missionaries in Canada, he accompanied his converts when they went on the warpath so that he could continue to oversee their spiritual instruction and discourage them from participating in what he considered to be pagan practices, such as torturing and cannibalizing prisoners. Roubaud accompanied Abenaki warriors who joined Montcalm's army for the siege of Fort William Henry in 1757. He witnessed the attack on the fort's soldiers and civilians after they had surrendered and described what he saw in a report to his superiors.

At the very dawn of day [August 10, 1757], the Savages reassembled about the intrenchments.[1] They began by asking the English for goods, provisions, in a Word, for all the riches that their greedy eyes could

---

[1] The fort's exterior fortifications.

From Reuben Gold Thwaites, ed., *The Jesuit Relations and Allied Documents*, (Cleveland: Burrows Brothers, 1901), 70:179–85.

see; but these demands were made in a tone that foretold a blow with a spear as the price of a refusal. The English dispossessed and despoiled themselves, and reduced themselves to nothing, that they might buy at least life by this general renunciation. Such complaisance ought to soften any heart; but the heart of the Savage does not seem to be made like that of other men: you would say that it is, by its nature, the seat of inhumanity. They were not on this account less inclined to proceed to the harshest extremes. The body of four hundred men of the French troops, selected to protect the retreat of the enemy, arrived, and drew up in a line on both sides. The English began to defile. Woe to all those who brought up the rear, or to stragglers whom indisposition or any other cause separated however little from the troop. They were so many dead whose bodies very soon strewed the ground and covered the inclosure of the intrenchments. This butchery, which in the beginning was the work of only a few Savages, was the signal which made nearly all of them so many ferocious beasts. They struck, right and left, heavy blows of the hatchet on those who fell into their hands. However, the massacre was not of long continuance, or so great as such fury gave us cause to fear; the number of men killed was hardly more than forty or fifty. The patience of the English, who were content to bend the head under the sword of their executioners, suddenly appeased the weapon, but did not bring the tormentors to reason and equity. Continually uttering loud cries, these began to take them prisoners.

In the midst of all this I arrived. No, I do not believe that any one can be a man and be insensible in such sorrowful circumstances. The son torn from the arms of the father, the daughter snatched from the bosom of the mother, the husband separated from the wife; Officers stripped even to their shirts, without regard for their rank or for decency; a crowd of unfortunate people who were running at random, some toward the woods, some toward the French tents; these toward the fort, others to every place that seemed to promise an asylum, such were the pitiable objects that were presented to my sight; nevertheless the French were not inactive and insensible spectators of the catastrophe. Monsieur the Chevalier de Levi[2] was running wherever the tumult appeared the most violent, endeavoring to stop it, with a courage inspired by the kindness so natural to his illustrious blood. A thousand times he faced death, which notwithstanding his birth and his virtues, he would not have escaped if a special providence had not watched over his life and had not restrained the savage arms already raised to strike him. The French

[2] François-Gaston de Lévis was Montcalm's second-in-command.

Officers and the Canadians imitated his example, with a zeal worthy of the humanity which has always characterized the Nation; but the main part of our troops, occupied in guarding our batteries and the fort, was, on account of the distance, unable to give them aid. Of what help could four hundred men be against about fifteen hundred furious Savages who were not distinguishing us from the enemy? One of our Sergeants, who had strongly opposed their violence, was thrown to the ground by a blow from a spear. One of our French Officers, in reward for the same zeal, received a severe wound which brought him to the gate of death; besides, in this time of alarm people did not know in what direction to turn. Measures which seemed dictated by the greatest prudence led to disastrous and sinister ends.

Monsieur de Montcalm, who was not apprised of the affair for some time, on account of the distance to his tent, came at the first notice to the place of the uproar, with a celerity [speed] which showed the goodness and nobility of his heart. He seemed to be in several places at once, he would reappear, he was everywhere; he used prayers, menaces, promises; he tried everything, and at last resorted to force. . . . In the meantime, the tumult was continually increasing, when happily some one thought of calling out to the English, who formed a large body, to hasten their march. This forced march had its effect; the Savages, partly through the futility of their pursuit, partly satisfied with their captures, retired; the few who remained were easily dispersed.

27

JAMES FENIMORE COOPER

An American Novelist Describes the Fort William Henry Massacre

1826

James Fenimore Cooper owed his literary reputation in large part to a series of five novels known as the Leatherstocking Tales, *all of which featured Natty Bumppo, a Daniel Boone–like frontier hero. Published in 1826,* The Last of the Mohicans *was the most popular of the* Leatherstocking Tales, *and several film adaptations of it were made in the twentieth century. In his novels, Fenimore Cooper combined historical events with fictional characters. His rendering of the Fort William Henry Massacre in* The Last of the Mohicans *was based on his reading of historical accounts, but it also reflects the romantic language and literary tastes of his day.*

As the confused and timid throng left the protecting mounds of the fort, and issued on the open plain, the whole scene was at once presented to their eyes. At a little distance on the right, and somewhat in the rear, the French army stood to their arms, Montcalm having collected his parties, so soon as his guards had possession of the works. They were attentive but silent observers of the proceedings of the vanquished, failing in none of the stipulated military honors, and offering not taunt or insult, in their success, to their less fortunate foes. Living masses of the English, to the amount in the whole of near three thousand, were moving slowly across the plain, towards the common centre, and gradually approached each other, as they converged to the point of their march, a vista cut through the lofty trees, where the road to the Hudson entered the forest. Along the sweeping borders of the woods, hung a dark cloud of savages, eying the passage of their enemies, and hovering, at a distance, like vultures, who were only kept from swooping on their prey, by the presence and restraint of a superior army. A few had straggled

---

From James Fenimore Cooper, *The Last of the Mohicans: A Narrative of 1757* (Philadelphia: H. C. Carey and I. Lea, 1826), 273–77, 281–82.

among the conquered columns, where they stalked in sullen discontent; attentive, though, as yet, passive observers of the moving multitude.

The advance, with Heyward[1] at its head, had already reached the defile,[2] and was slowly disappearing, when the attention of Cora was drawn to a collection of stragglers, by the sounds of contention. A truant provincial was paying the forfeit of his disobedience, by being plundered of those very effects which had caused him to desert his place in the ranks. The man was of powerful frame, and too avaricious to part with his goods without a struggle. Individuals from either party interfered; the one side to prevent, and the other to aid in the robbery. Voices grew loud and angry, and a hundred savages appeared, as it were by magic, where a dozen only had been seen a minute before. It was then that Cora saw the form of Magua[3] gliding among his countrymen, and speaking with his fatal and artful eloquence. The mass of women and children stopped, and hovered together like alarmed and fluttering birds. But the cupidity of the Indian was soon gratified, and the different bodies again moved slowly onward.

The savages now fell back, and seemed content to let their enemies advance without further molestation. But as the female crowd approached them, the gaudy colors of a shawl attracted the eyes of a wild and untutored Huron. He advanced to seize it, without the least hesitation. The woman, more in terror than through love of the ornament, wrapped her child in the coveted article, and folded both more closely to her bosom. Cora was in the act of speaking, with an intent to advise the woman to abandon the trifle, when the savage relinquished his hold of the shawl, and tore the screaming infant from her arms. Abandoning everything to the greedy grasp of those around her, the mother darted, with distraction in her mien, to reclaim her child. The Indian smiled grimly, and extended one hand, in sign of a willingness to exchange, while with the other, he flourished the babe over his head, holding it by the feet as if to enhance the value of the ransom.

"Here—here—there—all—any—everything!" exclaimed the breathless woman; tearing the lighter articles of dress from her person, with ill-directed and trembling figures; "take all, but give me my babe!"

---

[1] Major Duncan Heyward, a British officer and protector of the novel's two female protagonists, Cora and Alice Munro. In the novel, Cora and Alice Munro are the daughters of Colonel Munro, Fort William Henry's commander.

[2] The passage where the road entered the forest.

[3] Magua is the novel's major antagonist, an embittered Huron Indian intent on avenging himself against the British by taking Cora captive.

The savage spurned the worthless rags, and perceiving that the shawl had already become a prize to another, his bantering but sullen smile changing to a gleam of ferocity, he dashed the head of the infant against a rock, and cast its quivering remains to her very feet. For an instant, the mother stood, like a statue of despair, looking wildly down at the unseemly object, which had so lately nestled in her bosom and smiled in her face; and then she raised her eyes and countenance towards heaven, as if calling on God to curse the perpetrator of the foul deed. She was spared the sin of such a prayer; for, maddened at his disappointment, and excited at the sight of blood, the Huron mercifully drove his tomahawk into her own brain. The mother sank under the blow, and fell grasping at her child, in death, with the same engrossing love that had caused her to cherish it while living.

At that dangerous moment Magua placed his hands to his mouth, and raised the fatal and appalling whoop. The scattered Indians started at the well-known cry, as coursers [hunters] bound at the signal to quit the goal; and, directly, there arose such a yell among the plain, and through the arches of the wood, as seldom burst from human lips before. They who heard it listened with a curdling horror at the heart, little inferior to that dread which may be expected to attend the blasts of the final summons.

More than two thousand raving savages broke from the forest at the signal, and threw themselves across the fatal plain with instinctive alacrity. We shall not dwell on the revolting horrors that succeeded. Death was everywhere, and in his most terrific and disgusting aspects. Resistance only served to inflame the murderers, who inflicted their furious blows long after their victims were beyond the power of their resentment. The flow of blood might be likened to the outbreaking of a torrent; and, as the natives became heated and maddened by the sight, many among them even kneeled to the earth, and drank freely, exultingly, hellishly of the crimson tide.

The trained bodies of the troops threw themselves quickly into solid masses, endeavoring to awe their assailants by the imposing appearance of a military front. The experiment in some measure succeeded, though far too many suffered their unloaded muskets to be torn from their hands, in the vain hope of appeasing the savages.

In such a scene none has leisure to note the fleeting moments. It might have been ten minutes (it seemed an age), that the sisters [Cora and Alice] had stood riveted to one spot, horror stricken, and nearly helpless.

. . .

The cruel work was still unchecked. On every side the captured were flying before their relentless persecutors, while the armed columns of the Christian king [Louis XV of France] stood fast in an apathy which has never been explained, and which has left an unmovable blot on the otherwise fair escutcheon of their leader.[4] Nor was the sword of death stayed until cupidity got the mastery of revenge. Then, indeed, the shrieks of the wounded and the yells of their murderers grew less frequent, until, finally, the cries of horror were lost to their ear, or were drowned in the loud, long, and piercing whoops of the triumphant savages.

[4] In other words, an event that left a black mark on Montcalm's family name and honor.

28

HENRY BOUQUET AND JEFFERY AMHERST

Two British Officers Discuss Using Smallpox as a Weapon

1763

During Pontiac's War, Indians in the Ohio country laid siege to Fort Pitt, which the British had built on the site of Fort Duquesne. As Colonel Henry Bouquet marched a relief force toward the fort, he corresponded with his commander in chief, General Jeffery Amherst, in New York. Bouquet and Amherst knew that smallpox had broken out among the soldiers and civilians inside the fort and that its commander, Captain Simeon Ecuyer, had quarantined the infected in the fort's hospital. In these passages from their letters, Bouquet and Amherst discuss spreading the contagion deliberately among the Indians. Unbeknownst to them, while they were writing about this possibility, Ecuyer purposefully gave blankets

From Sylvester K. Stevens and Donald H. Kent, eds., *The Papers of Col. Henry Bouquet*, 30 series (Harrisburg: Pennsylvania Historical and Museum Commission, 1940–1943), ser. 21634, 161, 215.

and handkerchiefs taken from the fort's hospital to Delaware Indians as diplomatic gifts during a parley. There is no extant evidence that Bouquet pursued this idea further after he arrived at Fort Pitt.

[Enclosure in a letter from Amherst to Bouquet, July 7, 1763]
Could it not be contrived to Send the Small Pox among those Disaffected Tribes of Indians? We must, on this occasion, Use Every Stratagem in our power to Reduce them.

J[EFFERY] A[MHERST]

[Bouquet to Amherst, July 13, 1763]
P.S. I will try to inoculate the _____ with Some Blankets that may fall in their Hands, and take Care not to get the disease myself.

As it is pity to expose good men against them [Indians] I wish we would make use of the Spanish Method to hunt them with English Dogs, suported by Rangers and Some Light Horse,[1] who would I think effectualy extirpate or remove that Vermin.

[Enclosure in a letter from Amherst to Bouquet, July 16, 1763]
You will Do well to try to Innoculate the Indians, by means of Blankets, as well as to Try Every other Method, that can Serve to Extirpate this Execrable Race. I should be very glad your Scheme for Hunting them down by Dogs could take Effect; but England is at too great a Distance to think of that at present.

J[EFFERY]. A[MHERST].

---

[1] During the sixteenth-century Spanish conquests in the Americas, conquistadors used mastiffs and other large dogs to terrorize Indians.

29

BENJAMIN FRANKLIN

An Anti–Paxton Boys Pamphlet

1764

In two separate incidents in December 1763, an armed mob of approximately fifty Scots-Irish settlers from the Paxton region in the lower Susquehanna Valley (modern Harrisburg, Pennsylvania) murdered the twenty inhabitants of Conestoga Indian Town, an Indian community that had existed peacefully amid the colonial inhabitants of Lancaster County since the late seventeenth century. News of these murders ignited a pamphlet war in Philadelphia between critics and defenders of the frontier vigilantes. The opening salvo was an anti–Paxton Boys piece published anonymously in January 1764 and attributed to Benjamin Franklin. Franklin had attended Indian treaty conferences as a delegate from Pennsylvania during the 1750s, and as a printer, he had published several of Pennsylvania's Indian treaties. He described the Conestogas as poor but loyal friends of the colonists and the Paxton Boys as the real savages of the frontier. His pamphlet was one of the first to identify an incident of European-on-Indian violence as a "massacre."

These Indians were the Remains of a Tribe of the Six Nations,[1] settled at Conestogoe, and thence called Conestogoe Indians. On the first Arrival of the English in Pennsylvania, Messengers from this Tribe came to welcome them, with Presents of Venison, Corn and Skins; and the whole Tribe entered into a Treaty of Friendship with the first Proprietor, William Penn, which was to last "as long as the Sun should shine, or the Waters run in the Rivers."

This Treaty has been since frequently renewed, and the *Chain brightened*, as they express it, from time to time. It has never been violated,

---

[1] The Conestogas were descendants of the Susquehannocks, an Iroquoian-speaking nation from the lower Susquehanna Valley dispersed by warfare and migration in the late seventeenth century.

From [Benjamin Franklin], *A Narrative of the Late Massacres, in Lancaster County, of a Number of Indians, Friends of This Province, by Persons Unknown. With Some Observations on the Same* ([Philadelphia: Franklin and Hall], 1764), 3–6, 8–9, 12–13, 25–27.

on their Part or ours, till now. As their Lands by Degrees were mostly purchased, and the Settlements of the White People began to surround them, the Proprietor [William Penn and his heirs] assigned them Lands on the Manor of Conestogoe, which they might not part with; there they have lived many Years in Friendship with their White Neighbours, who loved them for their peaceable inoffensive Behaviour.

It has always been observed, that Indians, settled in the Neighbourhood of White People, do not increase, but diminish continually. This Tribe accordingly went on diminishing, till there remained in their Town on the Manor, but 20 Persons, *viz.* 7 Men, 5 Women, and 8 Children, Boys and Girls. . . .

On Wednesday, the 14th of December, 1763, Fifty-seven Men, from some of our Frontier Townships, who had projected the Destruction of this little Common-wealth, came, all well-mounted, and armed with Fire-locks, Hangers [short swords] and Hatchets, having travelled through the Country in the Night, to Conestogoe Manor. There they surrounded the small Village of Indian Huts, and just at Break of Day broke into them all at once. Only three Men, two Women, and a young Boy, were found at home, the rest being out among the neighbouring White People, some to sell the Baskets, Brooms and Bowls they manufactured, and others on other Occasions. These poor defenceless Creatures were immediately fired upon, stabbed and hatcheted to Death! The good Shehaes,[2] among the rest, cut to Pieces in his Bed. All of them were scalped, and otherwise horribly mangled. Then their Huts were set on Fire, and most of them burnt down. Then the Troop, pleased with their own Conduct and Bravery, but enraged that any of the poor Indians had escaped the Massacre, rode off, and in small Parties, by different Roads, went home.

The universal Concern of the neighbouring White People on hearing of this Event, and the Lamentations of the younger Indians, when they returned and saw the Desolation, and the butchered half-burnt Bodies of their murdered Parents, and other Relations, cannot well be expressed.

The Magistrates of Lancaster sent out to collect the remaining Indians, brought them into the Town for their better Security against any further Attempt, and it is said condoled with them on the Misfortune that had happened, took them by the Hand, comforted and *promised them Protection*. They were all put into the Work-house,[3] a strong Building, as the Place of greatest Safety.

---

[2] Sheehays was an old Conestoga chief.
[3] A public building used to house the poor.

. . .

Those cruel Men again assembled themselves, and hearing that the remaining fourteen Indians were in the Work-house at Lancaster, they suddenly appeared in that Town, on the 27th of December. Fifty of them, armed as before, dismounting, went directly to the Work-house, and by Violence broke open the Door, and entered with the utmost Fury in their Countenances. When the poor Wretches saw they had *no Protection* nigh, nor could possibly escape, and being without the least Weapon for Defence, they divided into their little Families, the Children clinging to the Parents; they fell on their Knees, protested their Innocence, declared their Love to the English, and that, in their whole Lives, they had never done them Injury; and in this Posture they all received the Hatchet! Men, Women and little Children—were every one inhumanly murdered!—in cold Blood!

The barbarous Men who committed the atrocious Fact, in Defiance of Government, of all Laws human and divine, and to the eternal Disgrace of their Country and Colour, then mounted their Horses, huzza'd [cheered] in Triumph, as if they had gained a Victory, and rode off—*unmolested*!

The Bodies of the Murdered were then brought out and exposed in the Street, till a Hole could be made in the Earth, to receive and cover them.

But the Wickedness cannot be covered, the Guilt will lie on the whole Land, till Justice is done on the Murderers. The Blood of the Innocent will cry to Heaven for Vengeance.

. . .

There are some (I am ashamed to hear it) who would extenuate the enormous Wickedness of these Actions, by saying, "The Inhabitants of the Frontiers are exasperated with the Murder of their Relations, by the Enemy Indians, in the present War." It is possible; but though this might justify their going out into the Woods, to seek for those Enemies, and avenge upon them those Murders; it can never justify their turning in to the Heart of the Country, to murder their Friends.

If an Indian injures me, does it follow that I may revenge that Injury on all Indians? It is well known that Indians are of different Tribes, Nations and Languages, as well as the White People. In Europe, if the French, who are White People, should injure the Dutch, are they to revenge it on the English, because they too are White People? The only Crime of these poor Wretches seems to have been, that they had a reddish brown Skin, and black Hair; and some People of that Sort, it seems, had murdered some of our Relations. If it be right to kill Men for such a Reason, then, should any Man, with a freckled Face and red Hair, kill a Wife or Child of mine, it would be right for me to revenge it, by killing all the freckled red-haired Men, Women and Children, I could afterwards any where meet with.

. . .

These poor People [the Conestogas] have been always our Friends. Their Fathers received ours, when Strangers here, with Kindness and Hospitality. Behold the Return we have made them! When we grew more numerous and powerful, they put themselves under our *Protection*. See, in the mangled Corpses of the last Remains of the Tribe, how effectually we have afforded it to them!

Unhappy People! to have lived in such Times, and by such Neighbours! We have seen, that they would have been safer among the ancient Heathens, with whom the Rites of Hospitality were *sacred*. They would have been considered as *Guests* of the Publick, and the Religion of the Country would have operated in their Favour. But our Frontier People call themselves Christians! . . . In short it appears, that they would have been safe in any Part of the known World, except in the Neighbourhood of the Christian white Savages of Peckstang and Donegall![4]

[4] Paxton and Donegal were two Scots-Irish communities on the Susquehanna River, near modern Harrisburg, Pennsylvania.

30

MATTHEW SMITH AND JAMES GIBSON

The Paxton Boys Defend Their Actions

1764

After their two attacks on the Conestogas in late 1763, a much larger group of about two hundred Paxton Boys marched on Philadelphia in February 1764. They intended to kill approximately two hundred eastern Delaware Indians who were being sheltered in the city and any colonists who tried to stop them. As the inhabitants of Philadelphia scrambled to defend themselves from this armed mob, Benjamin Franklin mediated the crisis. Two leaders of the Paxton Boys, Matthew Smith and James Gibson, agreed to petition the Pennsylvania governor with their grievances. Their complaints were hastily published, providing the most complete defense of the Paxton Boys' actions in print. Not long afterward, the Paxton Boys went home without further incident. No one was ever indicted or convicted for the murders of the Conestogas.

Inasmuch as the killing [of] those Indians at Conestogo Mannor and Lancaster, has been, and may be the Subject of much Conversation; and by invidious Representations of it, which some, we doubt not, will industriously spread, many, unacquainted with the true State of Affairs, may be led to pass a severer Censure on the Authors of those Facts, and any others of those of like Nature, which may hereafter happen, than we are persuaded they would if matters were duly understood and deliberated: We think it therefore proper thus openly to declare ourselves, and render some brief Hints of the Reasons of our Conduct; which we must, and frankly do confess nothing but Necessity itself could induce us to, or justify us in; as it bears an Appearance of flying in the Face of Authority, and is attended with much Labour, Fatigue and Expence. . . .

These Indians known to be firmly connected in Friendship with our openly avowed imbittered Enemies;[1] and some of whom have, by

---

[1] The Paxton Boys claimed that the Conestoga Indians, despite their peaceful appearance, had aided and assisted other Indians involved in Pontiac's War.

From [Matthew Smith and James Gibson], *A Declaration and Remonstrance of the Distressed and Bleeding Frontier Inhabitants of the Province of Pennsylvania* ([Philadelphia: William Bradford], 1764), 3–9.

several Oaths, been proved to be Murderers; and, who, by their better Acquaintance with the Situation and State of our Frontiers, were more capable of doing us Mischief, we saw with Indignation cherished and caressed as dearest Friends—But this alas! Is but a Part, a small Part of that excessive Regard manifested to Indians beyond his Majesty's loyal Subjects, whereof we complain: And which together with various other Grievances have not only enflamed with Resentment the Breasts of a Number, and urged them to the disagreeable Evidence of it, they have been constrained to give, but have heavily displeased, by far, the greatest part of the good Inhabitants of the Province.

Should we here reflect to former Treaties, the exorbitant Presents, and great Servility therein paid to Indians, have long been oppressive Grievances we have groaned under. And when at the last Indian Treaty held at Lancaster,[2] not only was the Blood of our many murdered Brethren tamely covered, but our poor unhappy captivated Friends abandoned to Slavery among the Savages, by concluding a Friendship with the Indians and allowing them a plenteous Trade of all kinds of Commodities, without those being restored, altho' a spirited Requisition was made of them; how general Dissatisfaction those Measures gave, the Murmers of all good People (loud as they dare to utter them) to this Day declare: And had here, infatuated Steps of Conduct and a manifest Partialtity in favour of Indians made a final Pause, happy had it been; we perhaps had grieved in silence for our abandoned, enslaved Brethren among the Heathens. But matters of a later Date are still more flagrant Reasons of Complaint. When last Summer his Majesty's Forces under the Command of Col. Bouquet marched through this Province[3] and a Demand was made by his Excellency Gen. Amherst of Assistance to escort Provision &c. to relieve that important Post, Fort Pitt, yet not one Man was granted,[4] altho' never any Thing appeared more reasonable or necessary, as the Interest of the Province lay so much at stake and the Standing of the Frontier Settlements in any manner, evidently depended, under God, on the almost despaired of Success of his Majesty's little Army, whose Valour the whole Frontiers with Gratitude acknowledge as the happy Means of having saved from ruin great part of the Province. But when a Number of Indians falsly pretended Friends,

[2] The Pennsylvania government convened a treaty at Lancaster in August 1762 with Indians from the Ohio country and the Six Nations. The primary topic of negotiation was the return of captives.

[3] In the summer of 1763, Bouquet marched troops west from Carlisle, Pennsylvania, to relieve the siege of Fort Pitt during Pontiac's War.

[4] The Pennsylvania government had refused a request from Amherst for men to join Bouquet's force in its march to Fort Pitt.

and having among them some proved on Oath to have been guilty of Murder, since this War begun, when they together with other known to be his Majesty's Enemies and who had been in the Battle against Col. Bouquet, reduced to Distress by the Destruction of their Corn at the Great Island,[5] and up the East Branch of Susquehanna, pretend themselves Friends, and desire a Subsistance they are openly caressed, and the Publick, that could not be indulged the Liberty of contributing to his Majesty's Assistance, obliged, as Tributaries to Savages, to support those Villains, those Enemies to our King and our Country. Nor only so, but the Hands that were closely shut, nor would grant his Majesty's General one single Farthing against a Savage Foe, have been liberally opened, and the publick Money lavishly prostituted to hire, at an exorbitant Rate, a mercenary Guard, to protect his Majesty's worst of Enemies, those falsly pretended Indian Friends,[6] while at the same Time hundreds of poor distressed Families of his Majesty's Subjects, obliged to abandon their Possessions, and flee for their Lives at least, except a small Relief, at first, in the most distressing Circumstances, were left to starve neglected, save what the friendly Hand of private Donations has contributed to their Support; wherein they, who are most profuse towards Savages, have carefully avoided having any Part. . . . When a Seneca Indian, who, by the Information of many, as well as by his own Confession, had been through the last War an inveterate Enemy had got a Cut in his Head last Summer, in a Quarrel he had with his own Cousin, and it was reported in Philadelphia that his Wound was dangerous; a Doctor was immediately employed and sent to Fort Augusta[7] to take care of him and cure him if possible. To these may be added, that though it was impossible to obtain thro' the Summer or even yet any Premium for Indian Scalps [scalp bounties] or Encouragement to excite Volunteers to go forth against them, yet when a few of them known to be the fast Friends of our Enemies, and some of them Murderers themselves; when these have been struck by a distressed, bereft, injured Frontier, a liberal Reward is offered for apprehending the Perpetrators of the horrible Crime of killing his Majesty's cloaked Enemies: And their Conduct painted in the most atrocious Colours, while the horrid Ravages, cruel Murders and most shocking Barbarities committed by

---

[5] In the west branch of the Susquehanna River; site of a Delaware town.

[6] The Pennsylvania assembly provided funds in 1763 to move Delaware Indians living among Moravian missionaries east from the Susquehanna Valley to Philadelphia, to protect them from assault by frontiersmen.

[7] A Pennsylvania fort built at the juncture of the northern and western branches of the Susquehanna River.

Indians on His Majesty's Subjects are covered over and excused under the charitable Term of this being their Method of making War.

. . . Such is our unhappy Situation, under the Villany, Infatuation and Influence of a certain Faction[8] that have got the political Reigns in their Hand and tamely tyrannize over the other good Subjects of the Province! And can it be thought strange, that a Scene of such Treatment as this, and the now adding in this critical Juncture to all our former Distresses, that disagreeable Burden of supporting, in the very Heart of the Province, at so great an Expence, between One and Two Hundred Savages, to the great Disquietude of the Majority of the good Inhabitants of this Province, should awaken the Resentment of a People grossly abused, unrighteously burdened, and made Dupes and Slaves to Indians? And must not all well disposed People entertain a charitable Sentiment of those, who at their own great Expence and Trouble, have attempted, or shall attempt rescuing a labouring Land from a Weight so oppressive, unreasonable and unjust? It is this we Design, it is this we are resolved to prosecute, tho' it is with great Reluctance we are obliged to adopt a Measure, not so agreeable as could be desired, and to which Extremity alone compels.

GOD Save the KING.

February, 1764.

---

[8] Quaker delegates in the Pennsylvania assembly.

7

Prophecies and Legacies

Formal hostilities between the French and British on mainland North America ended with the fall of Montreal in September 1760, but the Seven Years' War continued elsewhere around the globe and was in fact prolonged by the entry of Spain into the conflict as an ally of France in 1761. This move proved to be disastrous for the Spanish. In 1762, the British took Havana, the crown jewel of the Spanish Caribbean, and in that same year, halfway around the globe, another British force sailing out of India took Manila in the Philippines. Colonial Americans participated in the Havana expedition, where many succumbed to the tropical diseases that killed soldiers with far greater efficiency than enemy fire whenever European armies ventured into the Caribbean.

Britain's victories around the globe meant that there was great potential for reconfiguring the map of empire in the peace negotiations. Since the late seventeenth century, Europe's great powers had usually ended their wars by returning some conquered territories and retaining others, always keeping an eye on maintaining a balance of power among the belligerents. For this reason, wars that began over border disputes (as had the Seven Years' War in the Ohio country) rarely settled them definitively, and wartime conquests were often returned in the peace settlement. However, the success of British arms and the debilitating defeats suffered by France and Spain meant that Britain could press its advantages in the peace negotiations as it had never done before.

This was a pivotal moment for the British Empire. Before 1754, the British tended to think of colonies as entrepreneurial commercial outposts, funded and run by private individuals or corporations hoping to profit by exporting a valuable raw material such as fish, furs, sugar, or tobacco. Other than granting charters and regulating their trade, the British crown exhibited little interest in its colonies and expended even less money on governing or protecting them. The Seven Years' War changed all that. Fighting the war's overseas campaigns had doubled the national debt and sent thousands of British soldiers and sailors around the globe. Furthermore, conquests in North America, the Caribbean,

Africa, India, and the Pacific brought new dominions under the crown's authority and made their indigenous peoples nominal subjects of it. Ruling this global empire would require a thorough rethinking of British imperial policy.

Almost immediately after the fall of Quebec in 1759, commentators and observers questioned the significance of this event. As seen in Document 31, the inhabitants of New France, who had suffered mightily during the war, feared that they would be abandoned by their king and country to a cruel enemy. The Protestant clergy in New England interpreted the British victory very differently. In thanksgiving sermons, they saw the conquest of Canada as a joyous, divinely ordained event that would forever rid North America of the French Catholic menace (Document 32). Across the ocean in London, however, there were voices that advocated restoring Canada to France because they believed that colonies should be small, privately run, entrepreneurial ventures devoted to extracting resources (Document 33). What good was a colony if governing its hostile foreign population and securing it from the crown's enemies cost far more than the goods that could be exported from it? By contrast, advocates for retaining Canada believed that a tremendous opportunity awaited Britain in North America (Document 34). Free of the French and their Indian allies, British subjects would multiply there without bounds, creating a vast export market for Britain's manufactured goods. In this vision of the empire's future, the colonists figured prominently not as miserable laborers producing plantation crops, but as free and prosperous consumers of goods made in Britain or imported from its other colonial possessions.

While the debate over Canada was transpiring in Britain, the army faced more pressing matters in North America. War broke out in Cherokee country, forcing the British to divert troops to the southern frontier, where they waged two scorched-earth campaigns against Cherokee towns in 1760 and 1761. In the *pays d'en haut*, redcoats occupied former French forts, and British traders returned to do business there. Wherever the army built roads to access these posts, colonial settlers followed, using the security provided by the army to claim native land as their own. Indians objected to these developments. During their peace negotiations with Pennsylvania in 1758, they had insisted that the British soldiers retreat eastward after they had dislodged the French from Fort Duquesne. Instead, the British built the much larger Fort Pitt in its place. Commander in chief Jeffery Amherst also cut off the distribution of diplomatic presents to the Indians now that he no longer needed to woo them as allies. The high-handed actions of the British and their inability to stem the tide of settlers across the Appalachians ignited a pan-Indian movement of resistance. Inspired by prophecies of restored prosperity and power if they would separate themselves from the whites (Document 35), warriors joined in coordinated attacks on western forts and settlements in 1763 that temporarily crippled British power in the *pays d'en haut*. Pontiac's War, as this uprising became known, forced the British crown to keep thousands of troops garrisoned on the American frontier and to impose a prohibition on settlement west of the Appalachians that alienated colonial land speculators and squatters.

Historians have long debated whether the seeds of the American Revolution were sown during the Seven Years' War. It is true that British policymakers were never able to solve effectively the problems created by victory in North America. Paying soldiers, policing colonists, and pacifying Indians required more money than the British government had ever expended in America, and during the 1760s, its efforts to raise that money by taxing the colonists backfired repeatedly. Yet it is also important to remember that the American colonists were never more firmly attached to the British Empire or prouder of their status as British subjects than in the period 1760–1763, when an age of unquestioned British power seemed to be dawning in North America and around the globe.

31

HENRI-MARIE DUBREIL DE PONTBRIAND

The Bishop of Quebec Describes the Suffering of the City

1759

Most of the major battles of the Seven Years' War were fought over wilderness forts far removed from civilian populations, but the siege of Quebec in 1759 was different. For almost three months, the capital city of New France endured destruction unprecedented in North American military campaigns, and the population's deprivations were compounded by the poor harvests and lack of supplies that had plagued Canada since 1757. While the British celebrated the fall of Quebec as a providential victory delivered by a Protestant God, the French remembered it as an unnecessarily cruel campaign waged by the British. That interpretation is evident in a request made by Henri-Marie Dubreil de Pontbriand, the bishop of Quebec, for charitable assistance from his superiors in France.

[September 5, 1759]

In order to excite the charity of persons imbued with the slightest compassion, 'tis sufficient to expose the condition of Canada.

Quebec has been bombarded and cannonaded for the space of over 2 months. 180 houses have been burnt by fire-pots,[1] all the others riddled by shot and shell. Walls six feet thick have not resisted; vaults in which private persons had placed their effects had been burnt, shattered, and pillaged during and after the siege. The Cathedral has been entirely consumed. No part of the Seminary is habitable except the kitchen, where the Parish priest of Quebec, with his coadjutor, has retired. That community has suffered still greater losses outside the town, where the enemy have burnt 4 farms and 3 extensive mills belonging to it, and which constituted all its revenue. The church of the Lower town is

---

[1] Incendiary devices used by the British to start fires within the city's walls.

From "An Imperfect Description of the Misery of Canada. By Bishop de Pontbriand," in E. B. O'Callaghan and Berthold Fernow, eds., *Documents Relative to the Colonial History of the State of New-York* (Albany, N.Y.: Weed, Parsons, 1858), 10:1057–59.

wholly destroyed; those of the Récollets, of the Jesuits,[2] and of the Seminary are unserviceable except by extensive repairs. Mass can only be celebrated with any sort of decency in that of the Ursulines,[3] although the English use it for some extraordinary ceremonies. This convent and that of the *Hospitalières*[4] have also been much damaged; they are without provisions, all of their lands having been laid waste. Meanwhile the nuns have found means to lodge there, however indifferently, after having resided during the entire siege at the General Hospital. The Hotel-Dieu [Quebec's hospital] is greatly straitened because the English sick are there. . . .

The English . . . have taken possession of such houses in the town as are the least damaged, and even daily drive citizens from their houses, who, by means of money, having had some apartment fitted up; or confine them to such narrow compass, by the number of soldiers whom they billet on them, that almost all are forced to abandon that unfortunate town; this they do the more readily as the English will not sell anything except for cash, and the money of the country, 'tis known, consists only of paper. . . . The private citizens of the town are without wood for their winter fuel, without bread, without flour, without meat, and live only on the little biscuit and pork the English soldier sells them from his ration. Such is the extremity to which our best citizens are reduced; hence the misery of the people and of the poor can be easily inferred.

The rural districts furnish no resources, and are perhaps as much to be pitied as the town. Côte de Beaupré and the Island of Orleans have been wholly destroyed before the end of the siege; the barns, farmers' houses, and priests' residences . . . have been burned, and the cattle that remained, carried off; those removed above Quebec have almost all been taken for the subsistence of our army; so that the poor farmer who returned to his land with his wife and children, will be obliged to hut himself, Indian fashion; his crops, which could not be saved, except on halves, will be exposed, as well as the cattle, to the inclemency of the weather. The secret deposites (*caches*) made in the woods, have been discovered by the enemy, and consequently the farmer is without clothing, furniture, plough and without any implements to cultivate the soil and to cut wood. The churches have been preserved to the number of ten; but the windows, doors, altars, statues, and tabernacles have been broken; the mission of the Abénaquis Indians of St. Francis has been

[2] The Récollets and Jesuits were two missionary religious orders in New France.
[3] An order of nuns.
[4] Another female religious order in Quebec.

utterly destroyed by a party of English and Indians, who have stolen all the vestments and sacred vessels, have thrown the consecrated Hosts on the ground, have killed some thirty persons, more than 20 of whom were women and children.[5]

On the other, or South, side of the river about 36 leagues of settled country have been almost equally devastated; it contained 19 parishes, the greater number of which have been destroyed.

All those places, just mentioned, will suffer seriously, and are incapable of assisting any person; have no provisions to sell, and will not be restored to their ancient state for more than 20 years. A great many of these farmers, as well as those of Quebec, are coming to the district of Montreal and of Three Rivers, but find it very difficult to obtain relief. . . .

I attest that in this description of our misfortunes nothing is exaggerated, and I beg their Lordships the Bishops, and the charitable to make some efforts in our behalf.

---

[5] Saint-François was an Abenaki mission town destroyed by Rogers' Rangers in October 1759.

32

JONATHAN MAYHEW

A New England Minister
Gives Thanks for the Fall of Quebec
1759

News of the fall of Quebec in 1759 and Montreal in 1760 prompted civic celebrations and days of thanksgiving throughout the British colonies, especially in New England, where it was customary for ministers to preach sermons that explained the spiritual significance of such worldly events. Jonathan Mayhew was a minister from a distinguished Massachusetts family who delivered thanksgiving sermons in 1759 and 1760. Like

---

From Jonathan Mayhew, *Two Discourses Delivered October 25th, 1759* (Boston: Draper, Edes and Gill, and Fleet, 1759), 23–24, 57–61.

many of his contemporaries, he saw God's hand at work in the British
conquest of Canada, and he believed it would initiate a new era of peace
and prosperity in the colonies.

I am even still almost "as one that dreameth," when I think of the surrender of the capital of Canada, which is in effect the reduction of the
whole country. For it is morally, if not naturally impossible, that the
enemy, having lost this city, which is now in our possession, should hold
out half another campaign, against a force much inferior to that, which
his Majesty has already in North-America. Yea, it is almost certain, that
after taking the capital, laying waste to the country, burning so many of
the houses, taking or destroying so great a part of the stock, stores and
magazines; it is almost certain, I say, after this, that a great part of the
enemy, who pretend still to stand out, must either come in, and submit
to the generous terms offered them, or else, before another spring, per-
ish by hunger and cold, with their unhappy wives and children; which
God forbid!

. . .

We, I mean New-England, and all the British American plantations,
had never so much cause for general joy as we have at present; while
we see ourselves in so fair a way, under the blessing of providence, to
be wholly delivered from our enemies in these parts. Had the French
retained their power, and independency of us here in America, we might
be certain from more than an hundred years sad experience of them,
that they would still be, not only our enemies, but false, perfidious and
barbarous ones; and not only so, but that the greater part of the savages still instigated, as they are already infatuated by them, would be
our enemies also. Canada, even tho' the French should relinquish all
their encroachments, and retire within their old proper bounds, is yet
so near to us, that it is impossible for Frenchmen, retaining their power,
and their independency on Great-Britain, to inhabit that country without
being pernicious enemies to us, in peace as well as war. Of this we had
experience, much more than sufficient. We have sadly felt the effects of
their perfidy, and of long wars, with the savages, wholly owing to them.
   We have all along been more or less disquieted, often greatly distressed, by these our American enemies. And there was a time, not
long since, when we had considerable reason to apprehend what the
consequence might be, how fatal to ourselves, and the British interest
in America. We had some reason for this, whether we reflect how the

enemy conducted, or we ourselves conducted, at that time. When they had a strong chain of forts quite round us, and boasted they had us in a pound. When not only all perfidy, which is nothing new or strange, but almost all the policy, the prudence, the military spirit, and I may add, the success also, seemed to have fallen to *their* share! These things then look'd with a dark and threatning aspect on the British affairs in America, and consequently, in Europe also. But blessed be God, that the scene is so much changed! "The snare is broken, and we are escaped." The power of the French is now broken, at least here in America, and not likely to be recovered. Our heathen enemies have no longer cause to "shoot out the lip," to deride and insult us, saying, Where is their boasted strength? "Where is their God?" Even they must now confess that the Lord hath done great things for us, whereof they may also in time probably be glad, how sorrowful soever they may be at present. And having offered up our praises to heaven for these favours, we can [now] make no prayer more seasonable, than that God would be pleased so deeply to impress our hearts with a sense of his goodness, that it may never be effaced, but that we may always remain humbly and obediently thankful for it. . . .

If we should henceforth live as becomes fellow subjects, and fellow-christians, in the fear of God, and brotherly-love, still "abhorring that which is evil, and cleaving to that which is good," we might then reasonable hope to see ourselves established without any rivals, much less perfidious and cruel enemies, in this good land, of such a vast extent, and that our posterity after us will also be glad of those great things which God has done, and is still doing for us. Even they will "abundantly utter the memory of his great goodness, and talk of his righteousness," if we and they become, and continue, a willing and obedient people. Yea, we may reasonably expect that this country, which has in a short time, and under many disadvantages, become so populous and flourishing, will, by the continued blessing of heaven, in another century or two become a mighty empire (I do not mean an independent one) in numbers little inferior to the greatest in Europe, and in felicity to none.

We ourselves shall, indeed, be all gone off the stage long before that time, and "gathered to our fathers." But our posterity will remain. And I must own, if I may so express it, that I feel a strong affection working in me towards those that are yet unborn, even to many generations. As I think with great satisfaction and delight on the happy estate of good men long since dead; especially of our pious forefathers who first peopled this country, and underwent so many difficulties and hardships in this undertaking for the testimony of a good conscience, and during their abode here, so I delight in looking into future ages, and seeing, at least in imagination, the prosperous and happy condition of those that are to succeed us. . . .

. . . I cannot forbear fancying that I see a great and flourishing kingdom in these parts of America, peopled by our posterity. Methinks I see mighty cities rising on every hill, and by the side of every commodious port; mighty fleets alternately sailing out and returning, laden with the produce of this, and every country under heaven; happy fields and villages wherever I turn my eyes, thro' a vastly extended territory; there the pastures cloathed with flocks, and here the vallies cover'd with corn, while the little hills rejoice on every side! And do I not there behold the savage nations, no longer our enemies, bowing the knee to Jesus Christ, and with joy confessing him to be "Lord, to the glory of God the Father!" Methinks I see religion professed and practiced throughout this spacious kingdom, in far greater purity and perfection, than since the times of the apostles, the Lord being still as a wall of fire round about, and the glory in the midst of her! O happy country! Happy kingdom!

33

An Argument for Returning Canada to the French

1760

Almost immediately after the fall of Quebec in 1759, policymakers and commentators in Britain began debating whether Britain should return Canada to France in the peace negotiations that would end the war. Those who favored returning Canada to France believed that it could be used as a bargaining chip for retaining the Caribbean sugar island Guadeloupe, another French possession that had fallen to British forces. They argued that this expansion of Britain's sugar trade would be far more profitable to the mother country than the absorption of the Canadian fur trade. Also, as the writer of the pamphlet excerpted here explains, they believed that keeping the French in Canada would serve as an effective

From *Remarks on the Letter Addressed to Two Great Men, in a Letter to the Author of That Piece* (London, 1760; Boston: B. Mecom, 1761), 26–33.

check on any inklings for independence among the American colonists. Authorship of this pamphlet is uncertain, but the two most likely candidates are William Burke and Charles Townshend, both of whom were British officeholders with experience in colonial affairs.

If we compare the Value of the Returns [exports] of Canada, even whilst it flourished most by its Incroachments upon us, with those of Guadeloupe, we shall find them in no Degree of Competition. The Fur-trade, whose Value is before mentioned, is its whole Trade to Europe. But Guadeloupe, besides the great Quantities of Sugars, Cotton, Indigo, Coffee, and Ginger, which it sends to Market, carries on a Trade with the Carraccas[1] and other Parts of the Spanish Main, which is a Trade wholly in the Manufactures of Europe, and the Returns for which, are almost wholly in ready Money. Without estimating the Land, the Houses, the Works, and the Goods in the Island, the Slaves, at the lowest Valuation, are worth upwards of one Million two hundred and fifty thousand Pounds Sterling. It is a known Fact, that they make more Sugar in Guadeloupe, than in any of our Islands, except Jamaica. This Branch alone, besides the Employment of so much Shipping, and so many Seamen, will produce clear 300,000 per Annum [£300,000 annually] to our Merchants. For, having sufficient from our own Islands, to supply our Home-consumption, the whole Sugar-produce of Guadeloupe will be exported; and will consequently be so much clear Money to Great Britain. And, Sir, the whole Produce of Canada, though it were all exported from England, and exported completely manufactured, would not amount to the Value of that single Article unmanufactured; nor would it employ the one twentieth Part of the Shipping, and the Seamen.

But this, though the largest, is not the only Produce of Guadeloupe; Coffee, which in our Islands is none, or a very inconsiderable Object, is there a very great one. They raise besides, great Quantities of Indigo and Cotton, which supply Materials for our best and most valuable Manufactures, and which employ many more Hands than the Increase of the Hat-trade,[2] proposed by the keeping Canada, can do. This island is capable, in our Hands, of being improved to double its present Value;

---

[1] Caracas, in modern Venezuela, was an important seaport along the northern coast of South America.

[2] Beaver pelts, the chief export of the fur trade, were manufactured into hats in Britain.

whereas Canada, in our Hands, would not probably yield half what it did to France. . . .

To view the Continent of America in a commercial Light, the Produce of all the Northern Colonies is the same as that of England, Corn, and Cattle; and therefore, except for a few naval Stores, there is very little Trade from thence directly to England. Their own Commodities bear a very low Price; Goods carried from Europe bear a very high Price; and thus they are of necessity driven to set up Manufactures similar to those of England, in which they are favoured by the Plenty and Cheapness of Provisions. In fact, there are Manufactures of many Kinds in these Northern Colonies, that promise in a short Time to supply their Home-consumption. From New England they begin even to export some things manufactured, as Hats, for instance. In these Provinces they have Colleges and Academies for the Education of their Youth; and as they increase daily in People and in Industry, the Necessity of a Connection with England, with which they have no natural Intercourse by a Reciprocation of Wants,[3] will continually diminish. But as they recede from the Sea,[4] all these Causes will operate more strongly; . . . they must live wholly on their own Labour, and in Process of Time will know little, inquire little, and care little about the Mother-country.

If, Sir, the people of our Colonies find no Check from Canada, they will extend themselves, almost without Bounds, into the Inland Parts. They are invited to it by the Pleasantness, the Fertility, and the Plenty of that Country; and they will increase infinitely from all Causes. What the Consequence will be, to have a numerous, hardy, independent People, possessed of a strong Country, communicating little, or not at all with England, I leave to your own Reflections. I hope we have not gone to these immense Expences,[5] without any Idea of securing the Fruits of them to Posterity. If we have, I am sure we have acted with little Frugality or Foresight. This is indeed a Point that must be the constant Object of the Ministers Attention, but is not a fit subject for a Discussion; I will therefore expatiate no farther on this Topic: I shall only observe, that by eagerly grasping at extensive Territory, we may run the Risque, and that perhaps in no very distant Period, of losing what we now possess. The possession of Canada, far from being necessary to our Safety, may in its Consequence be even dangerous. A Neighbour that keeps us in some Awe, is not always the worst of Neighbours. So that far from

[3] In other words, no mutual interests in trade.
[4] As colonists settle farther west.
[5] Of establishing the colonies and defending them from their enemies.

sacrificing Guadeloupe to Canada, perhaps, if we might have Canada without any Sacrifice at all, we ought not to desire it. And, besides the Points to be considered between us and France, there are other Powers who will probably think themselves interested in the Decision of this Affair. There is a Balance of Power in America as well as in Europe, which will not be forgotten; and *this is a Point I should have expected would somewhat have engaged your Attention.*

34

BENJAMIN FRANKLIN

An Argument against Restoring Canada to the French

1760

Benjamin Franklin was living in London as an agent for the Pennsylvania assembly when the Canada debate broke out in the press. He published an anonymous pamphlet responding directly to the argument made for giving Canada back to the French in the previous document, and it was quickly reprinted in America. As was the case with many colonial Americans, the war had inspired in Franklin a sense of patriotic attachment to Britain, and he believed that the Americans' wartime sacrifices had cemented a new partnership between them and their fellow subjects across the Atlantic. He wrote this pamphlet to assert the colonists' place within the empire and to assuage any concerns in Britain that they might be inclined toward independence.

If the French remain in Canada and Louisiana, fix the boundaries as you will between us and them, we must border on each other for more than 1500 miles. The people that inhabit the frontiers, are generally the refuse of both nations, often of the worst morals and the least discretion,

From [Benjamin Franklin], *The Interest of Great Britain Considered, with Regard to Her Colonies, and the Acquisitions of Canada and Guadaloupe* (Philadelphia: William Bradford, 1760), 8–9, 11–12, 16–17, 19–20, 31–32.

remote from the eye, the prudence, and the restraint of government. Injuries are therefore and frequently, in some part or other of so long a frontier, committed on both sides, resentment provoked, the colonies first engaged, and then the mother countries. And two great nations can scarce be at war in Europe, but some other prince or state thinks it a convenient opportunity, to revive some ancient claim, seize some advantage, obtain some territory, or enlarge some power at the expence of a neighbour. The flames of war once kindled, often spread far and wide, and the mischief is infinite. . . . Nor is it to be wondered at that people of different language, religion, and manners, should in those remote parts engage in frequent quarrels, when we find, that even the people of our own colonies have frequently been so exasperated against each other in their disputes about boundaries, as to proceed to open violence and bloodshed.

. . .

During a peace, it is not to be doubted the French, who are adroit at fortifying, will likewise erect forts in the most advantageous places of the country we leave them, which will make it more difficult than ever to be reduc'd in case of another war. We know by the experience of this war, how extremely difficult it is to march an army thro' the American woods, with its necessary cannon and stores, sufficient to reduce a very slight fort. The accounts at the treasury will tell you what amazing sums we have necessarily spent in the expeditions against two very trifling forts, Duquesne and Crown Point.[1] While the French retain their influence over the Indians, they can easily keep our long extended frontier in continual alarm, by a very few of those people; and with a small number of regulars and militia, in such a country, we find they can keep an army of ours in full employ for several years. We therefore shall not need to be told by our colonies, that if we leave Canada, however circumscrib'd, to the French, "*We have done nothing*"; we shall soon be made sensible ourselves of this truth, and to our cost. . . .

Our North American colonies are to be considered as the frontier of the British empire on that side.[2] The frontier of any dominion being attack'd, it becomes not merely "*the cause*" of the people immediately affected, (the inhabitants of that frontier) but properly "*the cause*" of the whole body. Where the frontier people owe and pay obedience, there they have a right to look for protection. No political proposition is better established than this. It is therefore invidious to represent the "blood

---

[1] Fort Saint-Frédéric at Crown Point, north of Ticonderoga.
[2] The western side of the Atlantic Ocean.

and treasure" spent in this war, as spent in "the cause of the colonies" only, and that they are "absurd and ungrateful" if they think we have done nothing unless we "make conquests for them," and reduce Canada to gratify their "vain ambition," &c. It will not be a conquest for them, nor gratify any vain ambition of theirs. It will be a conquest for the whole, and all our people will, in the increase of trade and the ease of taxes, find the advantage of it. Should we be obliged at any time to make a war for the protection of our commerce, and to secure the exportation of our manufactures, would it be fair to represent such a war merely as blood and treasure spent in the cause of the weavers of Yorkshire, Norwich, or the West, the cutlers of Sheffield, or the button-makers of Birmingham? I hope it will appear before I end these sheets, that if ever there was a *national war*, this is truly such a one: a war in which the interest of the *whole* nation is directly and fundamentally concerned.

. . .

I agree with the gentleman,[3] that with Canada in our possession, our people in America will increase amazingly. I know that their common rate of increase, where they are not molested by the enemy, is doubling their numbers every twenty five years by natural generation only, exclusive of the accession of foreigners. I think this increase continuing, would probably in a century more, make the number of British subjects on that side [of] the water more numerous than they now are on this; but I am far from entertaining on that account, any fears of their becoming either *useless* or *dangerous* to us; and I look on those fears, to be merely imaginary and without any probable foundation. . . .

The remarker thinks that our people in America, "finding no check from Canada would extend themselves almost without bounds into the inland parts, and increase infinitely from all causes." The very reason he assigns for their so extending, and which is indeed the true one, their being "invited to it by the pleasantness, fertility and plenty of the country," may satisfy us, that this extension will continue to proceed as long as there remains any pleasant fertile country within their reach. And if we even suppose them confin'd by the waters of the Mississippi westward, and by those of St. Laurence and the lakes to the northward, yet still we shall leave them room enough to increase even in the *sparse* manner of settling now practis'd there, till they amount to perhaps a hundred millions of souls. This must take some centuries to fulfill, and in the mean time, this nation must necessarily supply them with the manufactures they consume, because the new settlers will be employ'd

---

[3] The anonymous author of the pamphlet to which Franklin was responding.

in agriculture, and the new settlements will so continually draw off the spare hands from the old, that our present colonies will not, during the period we have mention'd find themselves in a condition to manufacture even for their own inhabitants, to any considerable degree, much less for those who are settling behind them. Thus our *trade* must, till that country becomes as fully peopled as England, that is for centuries to come, be continually increasing, and with it our naval power; because the ocean is between us and them, and our ships and seamen must increase as that trade increases. . . .

Thus much as to the apprehension of our colonies becoming *useless* to us. I shall next consider the other supposition, that their growth may render them *dangerous*. Of this I own, I have not the least conception, when I consider that we have already fourteen separate governments on the maritime coast of the continent,[4] and if we extend our settlements shall probably have as many more behind them on the inland side. Those we now have, are not only under different governors, but have different forms of government, different laws, different interests, and some of them different religious persuasions and different manners. Their jealousy of each other is so great that however necessary an union of the colonies has long been, for their common defence and security against their enemies, and how sensible soever each colony has been of that necessity, yet they have never been able to effect such an union among themselves, nor even to agree in requesting the mother country to establish it for them. Nothing but the immediate command of the crown has been able to produce even the imperfect union but lately seen there, of the forces of some colonies. If they could not agree to unite for their defence against the French and Indians, who were perpetually harassing their settlements, burning their villages, and murdering their people; can it reasonably be supposed there is any danger of their uniting against their own nation, which protects and encourages them, with which they have so many connections and ties of blood, interest and affection, and which is well known they all love much more than they love one another? In short, there are so many causes that must operate to prevent it, that I will venture to say, an union amongst them for such a purpose is not merely improbable, it is impossible; and if the union of the whole is impossible, the attempt of a part must be madness: as those colonies that did not join the rebellion, would join the mother country in suppressing it.

When I say such an union is impossible, I mean without the most grievous tyranny and oppression. People who have property in a

---

[4] The thirteen colonies that would rebel in 1775 plus Nova Scotia.

country which they may lose, and privileges which they may endanger; are generally dispos'd to be quiet; and even to bear much, rather than hazard all. While the government is mild and just, while important civil and religious rights are secure, such subjects will be dutiful and obedient. The waves do not rise, but when the winds blow.

35

NEOLIN

*A Delaware Prophet's Vision
for Renewing Indian Power*

1763

Not long after the fall of New France in 1760, a Delaware prophet named Neolin emerged in the Ohio country, preaching a message of spiritual renewal and Indian unity against the British soldiers and traders then occupying the former French forts in the pays d'en haut. *Neolin told his adherents that if they rejected alcohol, eliminated their dependence on trade goods, and lived separately from whites, they would be able to keep the British from seizing their land. His most famous follower was an Ottawa war chief named Pontiac, for whom the widespread war that Indians fought against the British in 1763 is named. A French trader named Robert Navarre recorded the most complete version of Neolin's message when he heard Pontiac describe it in a speech he made in 1763.*

An Indian of the Wolf nation [the Delawares], eager to make the acquaintance of the Master of Life, this is the name for God among all the Indians, resolved to undertake the journey to Paradise, where he knew He resided, without the knowledge of any of his tribe or village. But the question was how to succeed in his purpose and find the way thither. Not knowing anyone who had been there and was thus able to teach him the road, he had recourse to incantation in the hope of deriving some good augury from his trance. As a rule all the Indians, even those

---

From Clarence Monroe Burton and M. Agnes Burton, eds., *Journal of Pontiac's Conspiracy, 1763* (Detroit: Speaker-Hines, 1912), 22–32.

who are enlightened, are subject to superstition, and put a good deal of credence in their dreams and those things which one has a good deal of trouble to wean them from. This episode will be proof of what I say.

This Wolf Indian in his dream imagined that he had only to set out and by dint of traveling would arrive at the celestial dwelling. This he did the next day. Early in the morning he arose and equipped himself for a hunting journey, not forgetting to take provisions and ammunition, and a big kettle. Behold him then setting out like that on his journey to Heaven to see the Master of Life.

The first seven days of his journey were quite favorable to his plans; he walked on without growing discouraged, always with a firm belief that he would arrive at his destination, and eight days went by without his encountering anything which could hinder him in his desire. . . .

. . . Suddenly he saw before him what appeared to be a mountain of marvellous whiteness and he stopped, overcome with astonishment. Nevertheless, he again advanced, firmly determined to see what this mountain could be, but when he arrived at the foot of it he no longer saw any road and was sad. At this juncture, not knowing what to do to continue his way, he looked around in all directions and finally saw a woman of this mountain, of radiant Beauty, whose garments dimmed the whiteness of the snow. And she was seated.

This woman addressed him in his own tongue: "Thou appearest to me surprised not to find any road to lead thee where thou wishest to go. I know that for a long while thou hast been desirous of seeing the Master of Life and of speaking with him; that is why thou hast undertaken this journey to see him. The road which leads to his abode is over the mountain, and to ascend it thou must forsake all that thou hast with thee, and disrobe completely, and leave all thy trappings and clothing at the foot of the mountain. No one shall harm thee; go and bathe thyself in a river which I shall show thee, and then thou shalt ascend."

The Wolf was careful to obey the words of the woman, but one difficulty yet confronted him, namely, to know how to reach the top of the mountain which was perpendicular, pathless, and smooth as ice. He questioned this woman how one should go about climbing up, and she replied that if he was really anxious to see the Master of Life he would have to ascend, helping himself only with his hand and his left foot. This appeared to him impossible, but encouraged by the woman he set about it and succeeded by dint of effort.

When he reached the top he was greatly astonished not to see anyone; the woman had disappeared, and he found himself alone without a guide. At his right were three villages which confronted him; he did not know them for they seemed of different construction from his own, prettier and more orderly in appearance. After he had pondered some time over what he ought to do, he set out toward the village which seemed to him the most attractive, and covered half the distance from the top of the mountain before he remembered that he was naked. He was afraid to go further, but he heard a voice telling him to continue and that he ought not to fear, because, having bathed as he had, he could go on in assurance. He had no more difficulty in continuing up to a spot which seemed to him to be the gate of the village, and here he stopped, waiting for it to open so he could enter. While he was observing the outward beauty of this village the gate opened, and he saw coming toward him a handsome man, clothed all in white, who took him by the hand and told him that he was going to satisfy him and let him talk with the Master of Life. The Wolf permitted the man to conduct him, and both came to a place of surpassing beauty which the Indian could not admire enough. Here he saw the Master of Life who took him by the hand and gave him a hat all bordered with gold to sit down upon. The Wolf hesitated to do this for fear of spoiling the hat, but he was ordered to do so, and obeyed without reply.

After the Indian was seated the Lord said to him: "I am the Master of Life, and since I know what thou desirest to know, and to whom thou wishest to speak, listen well to what I am going to say to thee and to all the Indians:

"I am He who hath created the heavens and the earth, the trees, lakes, rivers, all men, and all that thou seest and hast seen upon the earth. Because I love you, you must do what I say and love, and not do what I hate. I do not love that you should drink to the point of madness, as you do; and I do not like that you should fight one another. You take two wives, or run after the wives of others; you do not well, and I hate that. You ought to have but one wife, and keep her till death. When you wish to go to war, you conjure and resort to the medicine dance, believing that you speak to me; you are mistaken, it is to Manitou that you speak, an evil spirit who prompts you to nothing but wrong, and who listens to you out of ignorance of me.

"This land where you dwell I have made for you and not for others. Whence comes it that you permit the Whites upon your lands? Can you not live without them? I know that those whom you call the children of your Great Father[1] supply your needs, but if you were not evil, as you are, you could surely do without them. You could live as you did

---

[1] The Indians of the Ohio country referred to the governor-general of New France by this term. After the British conquest of Canada, they used it to refer to the British king and his agents.

live before knowing them, before those whom you call your brothers [Europeans] had come upon your lands. Did you not live by the bow and arrow? You had no need of gun or powder, or anything else, and nevertheless you caught animals to live upon and to dress yourselves with their skins. But when I saw that you were given up to evil, I led the wild animals to the depths of the forests so that you had to depend upon your brothers to feed and shelter you. You have only to become good again and do what I wish, and I will send back the animals for your food.

"I do not forbid you to permit among you the children of your Father; I love them. They know me and pray to me, and I supply their wants and all they give you. But as to those who come to trouble your lands, drive them out, make war upon them. I do not love them at all; they know me not, and are my enemies, and the enemies of your brothers. Send them back to the lands which I have created for them and let them stay there. Here is a prayer which I give thee in writing to learn by heart and to teach to the Indians and their children."

The Wolf replied that he did not know how to read. He was told that when he should have returned to earth he would have only to give the prayer to the chief of his village who would read it and teach him and all the Indians to know it by heart; and he must say it night and morning without fail, and do what he has just been told to do; and he was to tell all the Indians for and in the name of the Master of Life:

"Do not drink more than once, or at most twice in a day; have only one wife and do not run after the wives of others nor after the girls; do not fight among yourselves; do not 'make medicine,' but pray, because in 'making medicine' one talks with the evil spirit; drive off your lands those dogs clothed in red [British soldiers] who will do you nothing but harm. And when ye shall have need of anything address yourselves to me; and as to your brothers, I shall give to you as to them; do not sell to your brothers what I have put on earth for food. In short, become good and you shall receive your needs. When you meet one another exchange greeting and proffer the left hand which is nearest the heart.

"In all things I command thee to repeat every morning and night the prayer which I have given thee."

The Wolf promised to do faithfully what the Master of Life told him, and that he would recommend it well to the Indians, and that the Master of Life would be pleased with them. Then the same man who had led him by the hand came to get him and conducted him to the foot of the mountain where he told him to take his outfit again and return to his village. The Wolf did this, and upon his arrival the members of his tribe and village were greatly surprised, for they did not know what had become of him, and they asked where he had been. As he was enjoined not to speak to anybody before he had talked with the chief of his village, he made a sign with his hand that he had come from on high. Upon entering the village he went straight to the cabin of the chief to whom he gave what had been given to him, namely, the prayer and the law which the Master of Life had given him.

This adventure was soon noised about among the people of the whole village who came to hear the message of the Master of Life, and then went to carry it to the neighboring villages. The members of these villages came to see the pretended traveler, and the news was spread from village to village and finally reached Pontiac. He believed all this, as we believe an article of faith, and instilled it into the minds of all those in his council. They listened to him as to an oracle, and told him that he had only to speak and they were all ready to do what he demanded of them.

A Chronology of Events Related to the Seven Years' War in North America (1748–1763)

1748 Treaty of Aix-la-Chapelle ends War of the Austrian Succession but leaves Anglo-French border disputes in North America unresolved.

1749 Céloron expedition asserts French possession of Ohio country.

1752 *June* Pickawillany raid: French and Indian force attacks British traders and their Indian allies in Ohio country.

1753 *Summer* French build Fort Presque Isle, Fort LeBoeuf, and Fort Machault (Venango) along passage from Lake Erie to Allegheny River.

1753–
1754 *October–January* George Washington warns French in Allegheny region that they are trespassing on British territory.

1754 *Spring* French establish Fort Duquesne at Forks of the Ohio (modern Pittsburgh).

May Jumonville's Glen: Party of soldiers and Indians under Washington's command attacks French party from Fort Duquesne and kills Ensign Joseph Coulon de Jumonville.

July Washington surrenders to French at Fort Necessity.

Summer Albany Congress convenes to renew Covenant Chain alliance with Iroquois and drafts plan of intercolonial union.

1755 *July* Edward Braddock defeated on banks of Monongahela River.

Summer British capture several French forts in Nova Scotia and begin deportation of Acadians.

September Battle of Lake George: William Johnson defeats French attack led by Baron de Dieskau.

1755–
1758 French-allied Indians wage *la petite guerre* against colonists along mid-Atlantic frontier.

1756 *August* Marquis de Montcalm leads successful French siege of Fort Oswego.

September Kittanning raid: Pennsylvania troops destroy Delaware town on Allegheny River.

1757 *August* Montcalm leads successful siege of Fort William Henry; followed by Indian attack on garrison.

1758 *June–July* Jeffery Amherst leads successful British siege of Louisbourg, French fortress at mouth of St. Lawrence River.

July Montcalm successfully defends Fort Carillon at Ticonderoga from attack by British forces led by James Abercromby.

August John Bradstreet takes Fort Frontenac, French post on Lake Ontario.

October Treaty of Easton ends Indian war in western Pennsylvania.

November Forbes expedition forces French to withdraw from Forks of the Ohio; British build Fort Pitt on site of Fort Duquesne.

1759 *July* Fort Niagara falls to British forces commanded by John Prideaux and William Johnson.

September Fall of Quebec: British troops led by James Wolfe defeat French forces led by Montcalm on Plains of Abraham.

October Raid on Saint-François: American rangers commanded by Robert Rogers destroy Abenaki town on St. Lawrence River.

1759–1761 Cherokee War along Virginia-Carolina frontier.

1760 *September* Fall of Montreal: New France surrenders to British.

1761 *Summer* Detroit treaty conference: Johnson extends Covenant Chain alliance to Indians in *pays d'en haut*.

1762 *Summer* Fall of Havana: British conquer most important Spanish city in Caribbean.

Autumn Fall of Manila: British conquer capital of Spanish Philippines.

1763 *February* Peace of Paris ends Seven Years' War: France cedes Canada and all North American territory east of Mississippi River, except New Orleans, to Britain; France cedes New Orleans and Louisiana territory west of Mississippi to Spain; Spain cedes Florida to Britain.

Summer Pontiac's War: Indians in the *pays d'en haut* take up arms against British in protest of Amherst's Indian policy.

October Proclamation of 1763: British crown bars colonial settlement west of Appalachian Mountains until land purchased from Indians.

Questions for Consideration

1. Compare the advantages and disadvantages of the British and French colonial systems as they tried to assert possession of the Ohio country. (See especially Documents 2 and 3.)

2. How did the French and Indians describe their relationship with each other? What attributes did Indians expect Onontio to exhibit as "the Great Father"? (See Document 1.)

3. Describe the tensions among Indians, fur traders, settlers, and colonial officials over access to and use of western land. (See Documents 4 and 5.)

4. How did religion shape British perceptions of the French in North America? (See especially Document 6.)

5. Why did the Ohio Indians choose to ally with the French when war broke out in 1754? (See especially Document 11.)

6. Reconstruct the events at Jumonville's Glen and Fort Necessity from the British and French perspectives. Why do you think George Washington was so concerned with defending his actions there? (See Documents 7–9.)

7. Why was General Edward Braddock's army so quickly and decisively defeated as it approached Fort Duquesne? (See Document 10.)

8. Describe the rules and conventions that governed siegecraft. How did the presence of Indian allies complicate the implementation of these rules? (See Documents 12–14.)

9. What was *la petite guerre*? How did the French use it to compensate for their other military weaknesses in North America? (See Documents 13 and 14.)

10. Using Charlotte Brown as your example, describe how working for the British army both endorsed and challenged women's traditional gender roles. (See Document 15.)

11. Using David Perry and Robert Rogers as your examples, describe how New England soldiers reacted to the British cause. Where in Rogers's rules for his rangers do you see evidence of his blending of Native American and European tactics? (See Documents 16 and 17.)

12. What uses did Indians have for captives? How are those uses illustrated in the captivity stories featured in Documents 18–20?

13. What evidence is there in these captivity narratives that Indians treated male and female captives differently because of their gender? How did adopted captives learn the gender roles of Indian society? (See especially Documents 19 and 20.)

14. Of the captives featured in Documents 18–20, which ones chose to return to colonial life and which ones remained among the Indians? How can you account for those choices?

15. Why do you think British army officers insisted on the return of all captives, even those who did not wish to leave their adopted Indian families? (See Document 21.)

16. Describe the process of conducting diplomacy with Indians. What common elements of diplomatic ritual and protocol are evident in Documents 22–25?

17. What sorts of objectives and demands did Indians express in their diplomatic negotiations? How do these compare with the objectives and demands expressed by their European counterparts? (See Documents 22–25.)

18. Describe some of the common metaphors used by Europeans and Indians in their speechmaking. Why do you think European observers were so fascinated by Indian oratory? (See especially Document 22.)

19. Compare the French and American perspectives on the Fort William Henry Massacre provided in Documents 26 and 27. How do you think an Indian account of this event would have differed from these two accounts?

20. What evidence is there in these sources of Europeans suspending their usual rules of war to fight Indians? What different methods did they use, and how did they justify them? (See especially Document 28.)

21. In the debate over the Paxton Boys, what logic did Benjamin Franklin use to challenge their violence against the Conestogas? How did the Paxton Boys use loyalty to the British king to explain their conduct? (See Documents 29 and 30.)

22. Compare the two perspectives on the fall of Quebec offered in Documents 31 and 32. How are the religious differences between the French and British evident in their interpretations of this event?

23. What different visions of the British Empire's future are evident in the two sides of the debate about restoring Canada to the French? (See Documents 33 and 34.)

24. Describe the message Neolin received from the Master of Life during his vision. What instructions did this message provide for Indians regarding their relations with Europeans? (See Document 35.)

Selected Bibliography

GENERAL

Anderson, Fred. *The Crucible of War: The Seven Years' War and the Fate of Empire in British North America, 1754–1766*. New York: Knopf, 2000.
Brecher, Frank W. *Losing a Continent: France's North American Policy, 1753–1763*. Westport, Conn.: Greenwood Press, 1998.
Cave, Alfred A. *The French and Indian War*. Westport, Conn.: Greenwood Press, 2004.
Fowler, William M. *Empires at War: The French and Indian War and the Struggle for North America, 1754–1763*. New York: Walker, 2005.
Hofstra, Warren R., ed. *Cultures in Conflict: The Seven Years' War in North America*. Lanham, Md.: Rowman and Littlefield, 2007.
Jennings, Francis. *Empire of Fortune: Crowns, Colonies, and Tribes in the Seven Years War in America*. New York: W. W. Norton, 1988.
Lenman, Bruce. *Britain's Colonial Wars, 1688–1783*. Harlow, U.K.: Longman, 2001.
Mapp, Paul W. *The Elusive West and the Contest for Empire, 1713–1763*. Chapel Hill: University of North Carolina Press, 2011.

THE OHIO COUNTRY AND *PAYS D'EN HAUT*

Calloway, Colin G. *The Shawnees and the War for America*. New York: Penguin, 2007.
Dixon, David. "A High Wind Rising: George Washington, Fort Necessity, and the Ohio Country Indians." *Pennsylvania History* 72 (Summer 2007): 333–53.
Dowd, Gregory Evans. *A Spirited Resistance: The North American Indian Struggle for Unity, 1745–1815*. Baltimore: Johns Hopkins University Press, 1992.
Furstenberg, François. "The Significance of the Trans-Appalachian Frontier in Atlantic History." *American Historical Review* 113 (June 2008): 647–77.
Hinderaker, Eric. *Elusive Empires: Constructing Colonialism in the Ohio Valley, 1673–1800*. Cambridge, U.K.: Cambridge University Press, 1997.
McConnell, Michael N. *A Country Between: The Upper Ohio Valley and Its Peoples, 1724–1774*. Lincoln: University of Nebraska Press, 2002.

Sleeper-Smith, Susan. *Indian Women and French Men: Rethinking Cultural Encounter in the Western Great Lakes.* Amherst: University of Massachusetts Press, 2001.

White, Richard. *The Middle Ground: Indians, Empires, and Republics in the Great Lakes Region, 1650–1815.* Cambridge, U.K.: Cambridge University Press, 1991.

WARFARE IN COLONIAL AMERICA

Anderson, Fred. *A People's Army: Massachusetts Soldiers and Society in the Seven Years' War.* Chapel Hill: University of North Carolina Press, 1984.

Bickham, Troy. *Savages within the Empire: Representations of American Indians in Eighteenth-Century Britain.* New York: Oxford University Press, 2005.

Brumwell, Stephen. *Redcoats: The British Soldier and War in the Americas, 1755–1763.* Cambridge, U.K.: Cambridge University Press, 2002.

———. *White Devil: A True Story of War, Savagery, and Vengeance in Colonial America.* Cambridge, Mass.: Da Capo Press, 2004.

Campbell, Alexander V. *The Royal American Regiment: An Atlantic Microcosm, 1755–1772.* Norman: University of Oklahoma Press, 2010.

Dunnigan, Brian Leigh. *Siege—1759: The Campaign against Niagara.* Youngstown, N.Y.: Old Fort Niagara Association, 1996.

Fatherly, Sarah. "Tending the Army: Women and the British General Hospital in North America, 1754–1763." *Early American Studies* 10 (Fall 2012): 566–99.

Fenn, Elizabeth A. "Biological Warfare in Eighteenth-Century North America: Beyond Jeffery Amherst." *Journal of American History* 86 (March 2000): 1552–80.

Grenier, John. *The First Way of War: American War Making on the Frontier, 1607–1814.* Cambridge, U.K.: Cambridge University Press, 2005.

Kopperman, Paul E. *Braddock at the Monongahela.* Pittsburgh: University of Pittsburgh Press, 1977.

Little, Ann M. *Abraham in Arms: War and Gender in Colonial New England.* Philadelphia: University of Pennsylvania Press, 2006.

MacLeitch, Gail D. *Imperial Entanglements: Iroquois Change and Persistence on the Frontiers of Empire.* Philadelphia: University of Pennsylvania Press, 2011.

MacLeod, Peter. *The Canadian Iroquois and the Seven Years' War.* Toronto: Dundurn Press, 1996.

Mayer, Holly. "From Forts to Families: Following the Army into Western Pennsylvania, 1758–1766." *Pennsylvania Magazine of History and Biography* 130 (2006): 5–44.

McConnell, Michael N. *Army and Empire: British Soldiers on the American Frontier, 1758–1775.* Lincoln: University of Nebraska Press, 2004.

Pargellis, Stanley M. *Lord Loudoun in North America.* New Haven, Conn.: Yale University Press, 1933.

Parmenter, Jon. "After the Mourning Wars: The Iroquois as Allies in Colonial North American Campaigns, 1676–1760." *William and Mary Quarterly*, 3rd ser., 64 (January 2007): 39–82.

Preston, David L. "'Make Indians of Our White Men': British Soldiers and Indian Warriors from Braddock's to Forbes's Campaigns, 1755–1758." *Pennsylvania History* 72 (Summer 2007): 280–306.

———. *The Texture of Contact: European and Indian Settler Communities on the Frontiers of Iroquoia, 1667–1783.* Lincoln: University of Nebraska Press, 2009.

Ranlet, Philip. "The British, the Indians, and Smallpox: What Actually Happened at Fort Pitt in 1763?" *Pennsylvania History* 67 (Summer 2000): 427–41.

Selesky, Harold E. *War and Society in Colonial Connecticut.* New Haven, Conn.: Yale University Press, 1990.

Silver, Peter. *Our Savage Neighbors: How Indian War Transformed Early America.* New York: W. W. Norton, 2008.

Steele, Ian K. *Betrayals: Fort William Henry and the "Massacre."* New York: Oxford University Press, 1990.

Stephenson, R. S. "Pennsylvania's Provincial Soldiers in the Seven Years' War." *Pennsylvania History* 62 (April 1995): 196–212.

Ward, Matthew C. *Breaking the Backcountry: The Seven Years' War in Virginia and Pennsylvania, 1754–1765.* Pittsburgh: University of Pittsburgh Press, 2003.

Way, Peter. "Rebellion of the Regulars: Working Soldiers and the Mutiny of 1763–1764." *William and Mary Quarterly*, 3rd ser., 57 (October 2000): 761–92.

INDIAN CAPTIVITY

Axtell, James. "The White Indians of Colonial America." *William and Mary Quarterly*, 3rd ser., 32 (January 1975): 55–88.

Colley, Linda. *Captives: Britain, Empire, and the World, 1660–1850.* New York: Random House, 2002.

Denaci, Ruth Ann. "The Penn's Creek Massacre and the Captivity of Marie Le Roy and Barbara Leininger." *Pennsylvania History* 72 (Summer 2007): 307–32.

Shannon, Timothy J. "King of the Indians: The Hard Fate and Curious Career of Peter Williamson." *William and Mary Quarterly*, 3rd ser., 66 (January 2009): 3–44.

Ward, Matthew C. "Redeeming the Captives, 1755–65." *Pennsylvania Magazine of History and Biography* 125 (2001): 161–89.

EUROPEAN-INDIAN DIPLOMACY

Merrell, James H. *Into the American Woods: Negotiators on the Pennsylvania Frontier.* New York: W. W. Norton, 1999.

Merritt, Jane T. *At the Crossroads: Indians and Empires on a Mid-Atlantic Frontier, 1700–1763*. Chapel Hill: University of North Carolina Press, 2003.

Oliphant, John. *Peace and War on the Anglo-Cherokee Frontier, 1756–1763*. Baton Rouge: Louisiana State University Press, 2001.

Shannon, Timothy J. *Indians and Colonists at the Crossroads of Empire: The Albany Congress of 1754*. Ithaca, N.Y.: Cornell University Press, 2000.

———. *Iroquois Diplomacy on the Early American Frontier*. New York: Penguin, 2008.

LEGACIES OF THE SEVEN YEARS' WAR

Bumsted, J. M. "'Things in the Womb of Time': Ideas of American Independence, 1633–1763." *William and Mary Quarterly*, 3rd ser., 31 (October 1974): 533–64.

Calloway, Colin G. *The Scratch of a Pen: 1763 and the Transformation of North America*. New York: Oxford University Press, 2006.

Conway, Stephen. "From Fellow Nationals to Foreigners: British Perceptions of the Americans, circa 1739–1783." *William and Mary Quarterly*, 3rd ser., 59 (January 2002): 65–100.

Dowd, Gregory Evans. *War under Heaven: Pontiac, the Indian Nations, and the British Empire*. Baltimore: Johns Hopkins University Press, 2002.

Faragher, John Mack. *A Great and Noble Scheme: The Tragic Story of the Expulsion of the French Acadians from their American Homeland*. New York: W. W. Norton, 2005.

Greene, Jack P. "The Seven Years' War and the American Revolution: The Causal Relationship Reconsidered." *Journal of Commonwealth and Imperial History* 8 (March 1980): 85–105.

Kenny, Kevin. *Peaceable Kingdom Lost: The Paxton Boys and the Destruction of William Penn's Holy Experiment*. New York: Oxford University Press, 2009.

Middleton, Richard. *Pontiac's War: Its Causes, Course and Consequences*. New York: Routledge, 2007.

Murrin, John M. "The French and Indian War, the American Revolution, and the Counterfactual Hypothesis: Reflections on Lawrence Henry Gipson and John Shy." *Reviews in American History* 2 (September 1973): 307–17.

Plank, Geoffrey. *An Unsettled Conquest: The British Campaign against the Peoples of Acadia*. Philadelphia: University of Pennsylvania Press, 2001.

Richter, Daniel K. *Facing East from Indian Country: A Native History of Early America*. Cambridge, Mass.: Harvard University Press, 2001.

Shy, John. *Toward Lexington: The Role of the British Army in the Coming of the American Revolution*. Princeton, N.J.: Princeton University Press, 1965.

Acknowledgments (*continued from p. iv*)

Document 8. From Donald H. Kent, ed., "Contrecoeur's Copy of George Washington's Journal for 1754" in *Pennsylvania History*, issue 19 (1952), pp. 20–22. Reprinted courtesy of *Pennsylvania History.*

Document 10. Charles Hamilton, ed. Pages 49–53 from *Braddock's Defeat.* Copyright © 1952 University of Oklahoma Press. Reproduced with permission of University of Oklahoma Press via Copyright Clearance Center.

Document 15. Isabel M. Calder, ed. Pages 183–88 from *Colonial Captivities, Marches and Journeys.* Copyright © 1967 Kennikat Press. Reprinted courtesy of the National Society of the Colonial Dames of America.

Document 22. Edward P. Hamilton, ed. Pages 8–12 from *Adventure in the Wilderness: The American Journals of Louis Antoine de Bougainville, 1756–1760.* Copyright © 1964 University of Oklahoma Press. Reproduced with permission of University of Oklahoma Press via Copyright Clearance Center.

Document 28. Sylvester K. Stevens and Donald H. Kent, eds. Pages 161 and 215 from *The Papers of Col. Henry Bouquet*, series 21634. Reprinted with permission of the Pennsylvania Historical and Museum Commission.

Index